Woodturning Book for Beginners

A Wood Turner Guide to Crafting 15 Woodturning Projects Plus Woodturning Tools and Tips to Get You Started

By

Luke Byrd

Disclaimer

This publication is designed to provide competent and reliable information regarding the subject matter covered. However, the views expressed in this publication are those of the author alone, and should not be taken as expert instruction or professional advice. The reader is responsible for his or her own actions.

The author hereby disclaims any responsibility or liability whatsoever that is incurred from the use or application of the contents of this publication by the

1

purchaser or reader. The purchaser or reader is hereby responsible for his or her own actions.

Table of Contents

Introduction

Woodturning is an art that can be pretty intimidating to most beginners. Seeing those complex equipment, tools and wheels could be the one thing that steals anyone's confidence, but then, this book will show you how simple the art is. I have decided to look at the principles of woodturning from the perspective of a student. So, together, we can deal with the nervousness that comes with turning a bowl on a lathe, sanding the edges of a project, and even cases where you have to bring down a project and start all over again.

That's why this book will cover several aspects like the safety precautions you will need to observe while using the lathe device. You'd think that working with a lathe needs no safety kit until you see your working space saturated with very visible dust particles. There will also be a guide in this book that teaches you how to get the right lathe device and the things you need to look out for to get that perfect cut.

Apart from cutting through wood, you will be taught how to sand wood, finish it, and other techniques that will give your project a wonderful look. For your practice are several project ideas that are great for beginners. Once you try out the majority of them, you'll see how better you'll become as time goes on. Lastly, you will also be graced with the opportunity of reading through a few questions other turners have had to ask as they went about with their turning projects.

With all of that being said and done, let's proceed to make some beautiful woodturning projects. The journey might be quite difficult, but then, with the right amount of confidence, you will scale through.

Let's jump right into it, shall we!

Chapter 1

Essentials of Woodturning

What is Woodturning?

Woodturning is an art that involves using tools and devices to cut through wood and to also mold it into different shapes and designs. This cutting process occurs while the piece of wood rotates along a particular axis—usually a horizontal axis—by a turner. The process of turning wood is traditionally referred to as turnery and the person in charge of the art is called a woodturner. When carrying out the process of woodturning, you have to possess a device known as the wood lathe. It usually carries out operations like sanding, cutting, knurling, facing, turning, drilling, and molding.

With this art, you could make several things like candlesticks, lamps, chess pieces, rolling pins, and other structures that can be carved out of wood. So, in woodturning, you will be carving out a symmetrical object out of an unsymmetrical one while driving the wood at high speeds using a motor-powered lathe and several other cutting tools to carve out designs.

History of Woodturning

Woodturning is an art that dates back to a thousand years ago. The major reason most of the wooden projects created back then could not stand the test of time is that the fibers of the wood are susceptible to rotting. They were only able to last a few years before they were eventually thrown out. Even with that issue, the turners then used a lathe that had no motor to power it. As pointed out earlier, woodturning is achieved when you use a lathe and cutting tools simultaneously. So, if nothing powered their lathe, how did they work? It was discovered that while they manually powered the lathe machines with their hands, they used their bare feet to hold the cutting tools in place. Can you imagine the degree of precision that the process would have required? For this very reason, most people did not take too much liking to the art at first.

In the period between the 500 and 1500 A.D, the first projects made by woodturning were discovered. They were found within the confines of ships like the Oseburg burial ship that had suffered wreckage at some point. Some other pieces were also found when wells were dug out where they were preserved in cavities that lacked oxygen. These pieces piqued the curiosity of people. What were those items? How were they created? Surely, there wasn't any tree that could birth such nicely curved pieces, so how did they come into existence?

That was how the art of woodturning was brought into the limelight. People got interested in it and in the 1500s, someone was able to create a flywheel that could drive the lathe. It was attached to the device with the aid of a drive belt. More people began to reason and a lathe device, driven by power sourced from water, electricity, and steam, came into existence after a few years passed. It marked a great turn-around for turners worldwide at that time as they got the chance to carve out the designs while holding on to the cutting tools with their hands.

Some other countries like Egypt, China, Arabia, and Rome had their lathe formulations. There was the bow lathe, the strap lathe, etc. As time went on, some other groups of people developed the continuous revolution lathe, the ornamental-turning lathes, etc. The advantage was that these lathes were able to cut through harder wooden plaques like ebony. And that characteristic was well received by the Princes of Europe. Ideas like wood molding, pattern making, etc., did not start until the period between the 19th and 20th centuries. Before the turners got to a stage where there was a lot of recorded precision, huge lathe devices that inscribed patterns in wood and scraping tools had to be developed.

But then, with all of the issues suffered in the past, woodturning has now become very common, safe, and lucrative. So many schools have inculcated the art into the curriculum offered at school and the students are being taught how to create beautiful projects from wood. Apart from that, art gives a huge sense of satisfaction and can, in several cases, save you time and money. You would understand how as you read on.

Profiting From Your Woodturning Projects

Before we venture into the details of woodturning, let's see how you can make money from the art. Do you know that apart from placing a piece of work in every room of your house, gifting friends and family, and other causes that would not necessarily fetch you money, you could also sell your works?

Making a huge profit from this art requires you to climb up the stage for beginners to that meant for professionals. Well, by the end of this book, you would have become one. Once you get to that stage where you can easily make art projects, you could even decide to make a living out of the art of woodturning. You could buy the fanciest cars and build the most beautiful houses, but first, you have to follow some already laid-down strategies.

- **What products do you want to sell?**

This question leads to several other questions that will all be attended to in this segment. First, let's see the first question that might arise. What project do you like crafting? You have to see to it that you do something that you enjoy! Making a living out of anything means that your whole life could be consecrated to you doing that thing. It must not be something that endlessly bores you to sleep. Imagine you sleeping more than you are working. How are you supposed to even make money? Luckily for you, there are several projects you can try your hands on. See what's best for you and work on that.

The second question has to do with demand and supply. Of course, you have to have target consumers. It could either be the young or the old, anyone! Are your products meeting their needs? Are you producing pens for the old? Do you think you will sell much in such an area? Selling things like chess pieces could be very lucrative. Old people tend to play with chess pieces as it helps them think better. You could also carry out market surveys to see what things your customers want. If your consumers like vessels with natural edges, selling vessels with round edges may not fetch you as much profit as you ought to make. Apart from the demand issue, let's see how many goods you can supply. The more you sell, the more money you make. If the demand is high, attack it with a high level of supply.

- **How do you plan on charging for your goods?**

This stage is where a lot of people missed it. They make beautiful projects, supply as many as possible, get excellent reviews from their customers, but unfortunately, they refuse to charge fees that will fetch them a lot of profit. So, in the end, even with all of their stresses and efforts, the money they make at the end of the day doesn't even cover the cost incurred in producing the projects.

Before you attach a price tag to any of your goods, take a little bit of time to estimate the cost of producing that item. It's very wrong if all you consider are the cost of the materials you used for the project and your labor. They are equally important factors, but then, other things like the cost of your tools, electricity, insurance,

14

and even the rent you pay for wherever you use as a work office should be considered. This method will go a long way to help you if you decide to make a living out of this art. You don't want to live your life settling bills, do you? No, of course not! And yes, consider the time you spent crafting out that piece. You could have easily settled for a movie with a full bucket of popcorn, but then, you didn't do that! Your customers have got to pay for that too.

Lastly, see that you attach a profit. You make a profit of at least 25% isn't too much. If after settling all the bills, you have nothing left to save, invest or spend, then, it is probably not worth it. Honestly, if your customers value your pieces, they would not mind spending a lot of money in purchasing them. Do not at any point sell your pieces at prices that would never pay you. That can be the worst scenario that could ever happen. Just see that your prices are not so exorbitant that no one even looks your way. Make them fair enough, but not at a very low price.

- **Where do you plan on selling your goods?**

After making those one-of-a-kind pieces of artwork, you can't just leave them on your work table, can you? You have to organize a way through which you can get people to see what you produce. If you don't have any idea of where you can sell your artworks, ask your fellow woodturners and know where they sell theirs. Attend craft shows, local shows organized by artisans, trade fairs, and so on. It may seem little at first, but then, the moment you get your first customer, satisfy him or her, and see how he or she will spread the news about your work. At some point, you might not even need to leave your house to sell anything. Your clients would come to find you where you are. Another place to sell your work is on Instagram and other sales pages like Etsy. Make use of this technology-driven world.

- **How do you plan on marketing your works?**

Marketing in the line of business involves anything that will help you to promote your business. What will get people to buy from you? What will get people to buy more from you? How do you plan on getting the world to know about what you have for them? The more you are known by people, the more sales you will make. To get quick and efficient results, you can pay marketing agencies that will help everyone become aware of the things you are offering to them. Don't let the price dissuade you. The results you would get at the end usually would complement it. You could also print sales cards, erect banners, share logos via WhatsApp and other messaging sites.

When marketing your projects, see to it that you pass across to the target customers the uniqueness of what you have to offer. Just make sure you come out differently. Give people a compulsory reason to try out your projects.

Woodturning job opportunities include;

1. Teaching other interested people how to practice the art of woodturning.
2. Writing books on the art of woodturning.
3. Selling projects like salt and pepper shakers, pepper grinders, rolling pins, wood trivets, salt cellars, bottle openers, honey drippers, jar lids, bud vases, Christmas ornaments, and other quick selling projects.

With all of these details, you should ensure that you take this art seriously. However, you shouldn't start with the mindset of making money. That could lead to you becoming too impatient and you might end up not taking note of the salient things. Start by making this art your hobby—something that you enjoy—then, continue in that same spirit. So, when it is time for you to make money, you'd not easily get tired of it. You know, there'd be a few times when things wouldn't go the way you want them to be. It happens in every business. So, you starting on the right foot will go a long way to ensure you don't get discouraged to continue in this art.

Chapter 2

Techniques in Wood Turning

The techniques used in woodturning is usually described by the nature of wood you use for the art. There are different kinds of wood available for crafting and each has its peculiar grain arrangement. The direction at which you rotate the lathe has to be in a direction perpendicular to the wood's grains taper to prevent issues related to wood chipping. Because of this reason, there are several techniques, with each one for a particular set of wooden plaques. Now, let's go through some of them.

Spindle Turning

Spindle turning is the commonest technique of woodturning and this is because of its simplicity. All you need to do is mount the wood between the head and the tail of the lathe machine before turning the spindle around. These techniques are several kinds of spindles and each one works for a particular kind of project. There's one that you use when making the stands of furniture and there are some other ones you use when constructing wooden pencils.

Decorative Spindle Turning

This technique's principles differ from the normal spindle turning as it involves processes like roughening, sizing up, and smoothening the surfaces of wood stock. Here, the wood stocks are cut out more delicately as there are many grooves, curves, shapes, and inner details that require a lot of precision.

Segmented Turning

Here, to form a plaque of wood, you would need to attach several pieces of wood before turning. Each wooden piece is fixed to the other with the aid of adhesives like glue. With this style, you could create stunning designs and patterns of cutting.

Faceplate Turning

This technique is different from the normal spindle turning method in that it is a technique that is done in a simple fluid movement of the wrist. This style allows the turner to exercise more freedom while using the lathe. For this technique though, you will need a faceplate. A faceplate is a metal plate in the form of a circle that is usually fixed to the end of the lathe. It will help in making your cutting faster by gripping the wood even more firmly.

The result of the faceplate technique are usually excellent as the turner can watch the processes involved in changing stock of wood into something more measured and symmetrical. Here, you don't have to join plaques of wood before turning it.

Bowl Turning

Professional woodturners mostly prefer this technique. Here, they use a bowl gouge to carve out wood into the shape of a bowl. To do this, the bowl gouge is held to the wood to carve out the insides. Apart from the bowl gouge, you will need scraping tools as it helps you to creatively carve out the insides of the bowl sharply and in a neat fashion.

Eccentric Turning

This technique involves the use of a single piece of wood. Here, you turn it around the lathe in different axes and planes each time to get your result.

Oval or Elliptical Turning

Here, while turning the wooden block, you might need accessories mounted on the head of the block as they work to alter the center at which the lathe rotates the wood through. This way, you get to place the cutting tool at a fixed angle of position while you cut out a shape that is more of an oval than a circle.

Sculpture Turnery

This turning technique involves working with a lathe machine that does not make only circular cuts but also cuts out more intricate shapes like ovals, triangles, squares, pentagons, hexagons, and heptagons.

Multi-dimensional Woodturning

In this technique, the wood plaque being worked upon while it moves along the lathe bed will rotate about certain axes.

Three-dimensional Woodturning

Anything three-dimensional has to do with something that has a length, height, or breadth. The shape produced from the woodblock is usually unsymmetrical about the axis of rotation.

Theming

In this technique, you will need to mount a carrier between two central points so that the axes at which the headstock and the tailstock cut through do not pass through that of the workpieces. This way, the workpieces get cut on only one of their faces. The term 'theming' was sourced from a Greek God, Hermes, who was often symbolized as a statue.

Green or Wet Woodturning

This technique involves a turner turning plaques of wood while it has a moisture content that is just above the point of balance, i.e., it is not too dry but slightly tipped towards the wet side. This technique is often carried out on fresh wooden plaques that haven't been dried in kilns. This technique might lead to you having to turn a plank of wood with varying levels of thickness, resulting in you getting work that isn't completely round.

In this technique, you could also try the rough turning procedure. Here, you turn a woodblock to a shape that allows your project to have a thickness that can dry your work back to the balance moisture values. The only benefit of drying your wood before turning through it is that a roughly turned woodblock will dry out more quickly but might end up breaking or splitting at the edges. Wet wood is easier to turn. They don't give out much dust and they also do not offer too much resistance to cutting tools.

Natural-edge Work

This technique involves working on wood with the outer edge linings of the trunk of a tree as the end of that piece. It is used majorly for hollow vessels like bowls. The final pieces may either have the barks attached to them or not. However, if you are going to leave the bark attached to the wood, you should ensure that it doesn't get damaged during the process of turning to get a completely beautiful piece.

Ornamental Turning

This technique of turning involves you mounting a wood block over a headstock while using a spinning tool to carve out intricate and decorative outlines. The device used for this technique is known as the Rose Engine lathe.

Twist Work

Here, the lathe, instead of cutting work, holds on to vessels and spindles while the turner makes the spiral cuts. The turner can make these cuts by using a grid outlined on the wood or by using either hand tools, power tools, or abrasives.

Chapter 3

Woodturning Tips and Tricks

In this chapter, we will discuss several woodturning tips and tricks that can help make your journey as a woodturner very seamless. Highlights of the most important tips and tricks are discussed below.

1. The tool rest of your lathe machine must be kept smooth. If the tool rest has rough outlines or pits, you can be certain those irregularities will be transferred to the edge of your cutting tool. And once that happens, your work gets ruined with a lot of disfigurations and crooked lines. To get rid of the holes, pits, and irregularities on your tool rest, you can use a mill file to smoothen the surface. To see that the tool rest remains straight and balanced around its ends, place a device with straight edges on the surface.

2. When making straight cuts on the rotating stock of wood, ensure that the tool rest is placed in a direction that is parallel to the lathe bed. To

ensure that the tool rest is in line with the headstock and the tailstock, you could depend on your eyes and sense of parallax. With that method, you can also check to see if the tool rest is parallel to the lathe bed.

3. Before turning on the engine of your lathe, roll the wood stock around its hinges through a complete revolution—360°. Also, ensure that the tool rest, tool rest banjo—the lathe component that holds the tool rest in place—and the lathe bed does not come in contact with the turning stock while you set it into a revolution.

4. When holding your cutting tool, see to it that you place it on the edges of the tool rest using the overhand technique. There are two techniques for holding cutting tool in place. There's the overhand technique and the underhand technique. The first one involves having your thumb placed in such a way that it grazes slightly over the top of the tool while you have your fingers at the bottom, supporting the tool. As you

do that with one hand (any of the two) —the other hand pushes against the back of the tool to ensure firm contact between the tool and the turning stock. This technique is mostly used for small stocks of wood and finishing cuttings.

The other technique is known as the overhand technique. Here, one hand firmly holds the tool down against the tool rest while the other supports the tool from beneath by pushing it slightly up to ensure that it makes contact with the wood stock. This technique is the one you should mostly work with as it allows your hand to press more firmly at the cutting edge and also, enables you to guide the tool better.

5. You could keep your cutting tool in place by holding it down with your hipbone. So, while you move the tool about the tool rest, you'd have to simultaneously move your body about too.

6. When cutting out a bowl with a bowl gouge, start cutting from the side of the wood that will form the insides of the bowl. To start, turn the flute

open and then turn it through an angle of thirty degrees. Starting your cuts with an open flute will prevent you from repeating the process where the gouge gets within the inner cavities of the bowl. Go on that way until you have cut out an edge that is adequate for the bevel to ride on. Then, you can now proceed to cut out normal lines with your flute.

The location of the bowl gouge flute depends on the direction the flute is pointed towards. Let's make reference to the direction of the hands of a clock for this explanation. When you read noon or midnight of a clock (12 o'clock), apply the way the hands look and turn the flute straight up. This arrangement creates an open flute. When you read off 9 o'clock or 3 o'clock, it means the flute is at an angle of 90° to the vertical. This arrangement signifies a closed flute. All you need to do to either close or open your flute is to turn it in the direction you'd see the hands of your clock pointing towards at that time.

7. Do not pass the tool beyond the boundaries of the tool rest. To ensure that, alter the position of your

tool rest and see that it is very close to the rotating wood stock before you power on the lathe.

8. For you to easily recognize your number one chuck jaw, mark it with paint. Marking your chucks will help you mount the wood stock on the hinges of the lathe in the same manner you removed it. Ensure that you place your markings close to the first marking on the chuck. The process where you realign and center your wooden bowl can be stressful at times, so it is necessary if you also get used to making small ticks or marks with gouges once you are done making a tenon. Doing that will help you easily find the center of the bowl if you later reverse the chucks.

9. For each chuck size, make a jig in the woodblock for chucks with the biggest-sized chuck and the smallest one. To ensure that the size of the hole you are cutting outfits into the chuck's opening, make a jig both inside and outside the wood.

10. When smoothening wood, run the abrasives beneath and across the side of the rotating wood stock before you shift the tool test away. One useful technique is to sand the wood from the bottom so that the turn marks are directed away from your fingers. If you are working with a lathe whose speed can be varied, you can smoothen the surface of the wood at a lesser speed. If the lathe moves in the opposite direction, sand from the top of the woodblock. To prevent a situation where your fingers get hurt, ensure that you shift the tool rest away before sanding.

11. Whenever you sand or turn your woodblock, ensure that you wear a nose mask and keep a dustbin close to you to help you collect the filings and dust. Failure to follow this guide can lead to issues with the lungs and other air passageways in the body. Use canister filters instead of bag filters. They work to remove even the tiniest dust particles from your breathing space.

12. Leave divider markings on your bench. The jaw chuck of size 4 exists in three different types. Each size has dimensions of tenons that it fits into. So, to make those exact holes in wood, you could just transfer the dimensions of each of the jaw sets to the wood. You don't have to do this procedure every time you mark a tendon as the chucks still keep their dimensions.

13. To get smooth, regular, and continuous cuts on the surface of a wood stock, you have to regularly shift the weight of your body. Moving your hands and your arms contribute to the process of cutting, but then, you moving your body as you cut contributes even more to the process. For projects like a wooden bow, you would notice that most of the curves and outlines come out sharper and neater when you transfer a little bit of your body's weight to the hands if you pay enough attention. You'd also notice that making some intricate curves and outlines will require you to move a few inches about. You cannot stay

at a point and expect your bowl to come out with a nice curve.

14. Wet greenwood. Greenwood can be very good for turning in that it can be cut out so thinly that having to dry it after doesn't pose any problem. Once it gets dry, the only issue is that the wood starts to have splinters or cracks due to friction stirred by the rolling lathe. To avoid this issue, you can choose to moisten the wood as often as possible to oppose the dryness created by friction. You could also dry the woodblocks slowly at reduced heat so that it retains a little bit of its moisture.

15. Try to follow your movements closely. Avoid distractions. For projects that need high degrees of precision, like bowls, you need to be careful of the tip of the bowl gouge. However, that isn't the only thing you should center your attention on. When turning wood, focus more of your attention on the uppermost outlines of the wood. This way, you'd be able to see how the outline of the vessel is being formed as you turn the wood.

16. Before mounting your woodblock on the lathe, see that you peel the bark with a screwdriver before you power on the lathe. The only time you should leave the bark in its stead is when you want to create a piece with a natural touch to it, or you need the bark attached for some other decorative purposes. If not, peel off the bark as neatly and carefully as possible to avoid ruining the main wood block. The reason for this technique is because flying pieces of bark being cut off a rotating wooden block can pose a lot of danger to the turner.

17. Before you sharpen the tips of your bowl gouge, make sure you color the bevel with a marker. Sharpening the tip of your bowl gouge will restore the original sharpness of the tool, not alter the shape. However, if the bevel is not inclined at the right angle before you begin sharpening the tip, what you'll get is a reshaped gouge bevel. To avoid this issue, mark the bevel with paint or

markers and then allow the bevel to touch the sharpening wheel slightly. This technique should correct the error across the whole bevel. If after sharpening, the mark you made gets peeled off from the bevel, it means the sharpener should be moved inwards. However, if the mark was removed from the bottom, you need to move the sharpener towards the back a little.

18. Make sure you have lighting that can be adjusted easily while you turn the wood. The light will help you focus on the too high or low sides or parts of the wood that have not blended with the other regular surfaces. It will also help you to sand the wood while following the grains in it. To see the cuttings made by a tool, shift the light so that it shines from the side of the bowl's surface. This way, you can easily see the marks, bumps, or scratches you need to smoothen out.

19. When creating a focus for a tenon, ensure that when it is seated, it does not rest against the bottom of the lathe's chuck. The dovetail joint of

the tenon must fit into that of the chuck. Lastly, ensure that the shoulder of the tenon is plane and square so that the edges of the chuck run smoothly through the surface of the wood with no irregularities surfacing along the way.

20. When cutting through a bowl rotated by a lathe, if it has a thin body, make sure you leave a mass of material in the middle so that it balances the piece as it rotates. Once you are done cutting out the edges at the top of the bowl, you can then move to the interior parts of the bowl and then cut out the central mass as you work your tool to the bottom. Do not try to go back to cutting the upper edges as you have now cut off the central mass that stabilized the piece.

A Short message from the Author:

Hey, I hope you are enjoying the book? I would love to hear your thoughts!

Many readers do not know how hard reviews are to come by and how much they help an author.

I would be incredibly grateful if you could take just 60 seconds to write a short review on Amazon, even if it is a few sentences!

>> Click here to leave a quick review

Thanks for the time taken to share your thoughts!

Chapter 4

Getting Started with Woodturning

Woodturning Tools and Materials

Wood

Wood is one of the important material needed in woodturning projects and there are several kinds of wood that can be used, with each having their own properties. See below for the different types of wood that can be used.

1. Ashwood
   - It is durable since it has high tensile strength.
   - It is resistant to hard falls.
   - It has a pale white color.
   - It has prominent grain lines.
   - The sapwood and the heartwood aren't easy to distinguish from each other.
   - It has an olive stain at its center.

- This wood is very suitable for projects with natural edges and outlooks because it is one of the few wood blocks that stick with their bark during the drying process.
- You can use ash wood to make bats, handles for hammers, shovels, etc.

2. Beech
- It is a bland wood.
- It has a distinct grain pattern.
- It is a pale wood.
- It is a durable wood that is resistant to scratches caused by abrasion.
- It has a reddish-brown heartwood.
- It has sapwood of a creamy to pink tone.
- It is a very hard and heavy wood.
- It has uniform and plain grains.
- It is very suitable for turning kitchenware as it doesn't affect the taste or flavor of food.
- Its plainness allows it to be perfect for the segmented turning technique.
- It can be used for making bowls, wooden toys, and for flooring.

3. Ebony
- It is a wood slab with colors that range from deep dark brown to jet black.
- It grows very slowly and gets to the stage of maturity after several years.
- Ebony is a very rare and expensive wood.
- Its deep black color makes it suitable for segmented turning techniques.
- Ebony can be used for cutting out black chess pieces and other dark carvings.

4. Hickory
- Hickory is the hardest of all the hardwoods available.
- It can deal easily with pressure.
- It has pronounced grain lines.
- It has an uneven color tone.
- Its sapwood ranges between white and cream.
- It has a tan or reddish-brown heartwood.
- It is resistant to shock and is very flexible.
- Hickory turns very well with the aid of sharp tools to cut through it.

- It is not too resistant to abrasion, so when running an abrasive across it, follow the grain pattern. If you go against that pattern, there is a big risk the wood ends up scratching.
- It is suitable for making furniture, parquetry, ladders, etc.

5. Mesquite
- It is quite easy to turn.
- It is not readily available.
- It has beautiful blemishes.
- Mesquite is suitable for pen turnings, pepper grinders, bottle stoppers, etc.

6. Rosewood
- Rosewood occurs in several forms.
- It is incredibly durable.
- It is a very good hardwood with a nice smell.
- It has a heartwood whose color ranges from golden brown to purplish-brown.
- It has its fibers interlocking into a nice design.
- It can be used to produce several magnificent projects like furniture, musical instruments, etc.

- The beautiful colors in which this wood exists make it highly suitable for segmented turning techniques.
- The dust obtained from cutting through this wood can be bad for asthmatic patients if inhaled.

7. Sycamore
- It has its grains woven into a nice pattern.
- This wood hardly splits or chips.
- This wood is plain.
- It doesn't alter the taste or smell of your food substances if you use it in constructing kitchenware.
- It has a distinct grain pattern.

8. Walnuts
- Walnuts have dark color tones.
- There are two types of walnut wood. There is the English walnut and the black walnut. The English walnut has a lighter color tone. The black walnut is durable and so, it is very suitable for projects like furniture and pistols.

- Walnut is very suitable for burling designs due to its grain pattern.
- It takes in glue nicely but if you leave the glue on its surface for a time longer than normal, there's a risk of you seeing a dark stain on its finish.
- Cutting through this wood will require you to use very sharp tools.
- The surface of this wood can be difficult to smoothen.

9. Maple
- It does not take finishing touches quite easily.
- During weather fluctuations, Maple increases and decreases in size reversibly. And because of that major reason, Maple is very prone to shrinkages.
- Maple is a strong and very durable wood.
- It has sapwood of a color that ranges between cream and white tones.
- The color of its heartwood ranges from light to dark brown.
- There are various kinds of Maple. There's the soft one, the hard one, the red Maple, etc.

10. Oak
- It has many grain lines.
- Its hardness will make your cutting tools get blunt quickly.
- If you place your cutting tool at a point of this wood for a long time, there could be the risk of it burning.
- There is a type of oak wood with a reddish-brown appearance and rough grains.
- How a project made from oak looks finally depends on the way the tree was milled when it was cut down.

11. Cherry
- Cherry has a straight and distinct grain.
- Its colors range from a sharp red color to a reddish-brown color.
- To carve this wood out unto the outline you desire, all you need to do is apply a very light force on the cutting tool.
- Its sapwood has a color that ranges from a yellow to a yellowish-white color.
- It has a purplish tone to its color.

- Its heartwood ranges from dark brown to purple colors.
- Cherry works well with oil finishes and lacquers.
- To smoothen the surface of cherry, you can use 400-grit sandpaper after it has become dry.

12. Poplar
- Poplar is a great wood for woodturning.
- It has a light color tone.
- It readily absorbs stains.
- It retains the color of the stain.

13. Pine
- There are two types of pinewood. There is the yellow pine and the white pine.
- The yellow pine offers more resistance to cutting tools than the white pine does.
- It is prone to scratches.
- It doesn't usually get dried enough for woodturning even when it is placed in a kiln.
- It can be used for making projects with a lot of patterns and moldings.

Lathe Machine

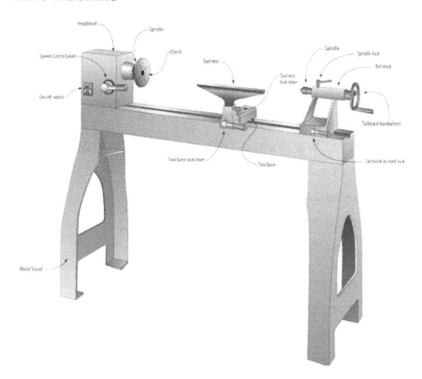

A lathe is used for operations like centering, facing, turning, knurling, chamfering, thread cutting, drilling, boring, reaming, pinning, tapping, etc. Two major types of lathe devices are used for rolling woodblocks. One is the free-standing lathe and the other is the bench-mounted lathe. The other types available are built with the idea of the two major lathes. Lathes have the following components and they are;

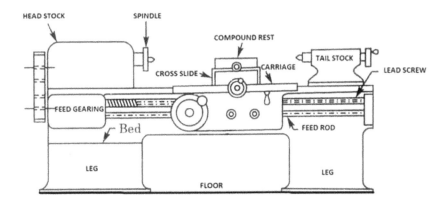

1. The on or off button: This is the button you press to power on or power off your lathe.
2. The headstock: This is positioned at the left side of the lathe machine and it houses the driving and electrical processes in the lathe. Its screws and spindle nose help in holding the wood blank in place. It also works to transfer power from the spindle to the feed rod, lead screw, and other cutting mechanisms. You'd find the following parts on the headstock.

- The 3-jaw chuck.

46

- The 4-jaw chuck.
- The lathe center.
- The collet chuck.
- The Faceplate.
- The Magnetic chuck.
- Gears.
- Feed controllers.

3. The tailstock: It is located on the right side of the lathe machine. It holds the tool for the operations you'd want to perform on your lathe.

4. The lathe bed: This part is the bed of the lathe machine. It is usually made from chilled cast iron. It is made up of two heavy metallic slides that run across the lathe's length. The lathe bed is very stank and can absorb large amounts of vibration. It bears the headstock, tailstock, carriage, and the other parts of the lathe.

5. Carriage: This part holds and controls the cutting tool. While cutting, it supports the tool firmly. It helps to transfer power from the feed rod to cutting tools. The carriage of a lathe is made up of the saddle, the cross-slide, the compound rest,

tool rest, apron, etc. The carriage pushes the tools in the following directions.

- Longitudinal feeding through the carriage.
- Cross feeds through the cross slide movement.
- Angular feeds through the top side movement.

6. The drive center.
7. Lead screw: This is also known as the translation screw. It transforms rotation motion into linear motion. You can use this tool for thread cutting operations in lathe devices.
8. The banjo and tool rest.
9. The speed control lever.
10. The tailstock hand wheel etc.

Types of Lathe Devices

There are several kinds of lathe devices and they are listed below with exact descriptions.

1. **Miniature Lathe**
- The swing is about 4 inches long.

- The length from the center of the lathe bed ranges between 6 inches and 12 inches.
- They are portable.
- This kind of lathe is used to turn small items like knobs and tiny toy furniture.

2. **Mini Lathe**

- The swing is about 10 inches long.
- The length from each center is about 13 inches.
- The engine runs at a power of about ½hp.
- This lathe is perfect for beginners and kids.
- The mini lathe is mostly used for the pen.

3. **Bench Lathe**

- This lathe is cheaper than most lathes that lie on the floor.
- This lathe can work with several kinds of projects.
- You can easily erect a stand for a bench lathe and then, adjust it to a height that corresponds with your midriff. Ensure that the bench you build is sturdy enough to withstand vibrations and pressure while you work.

4. **Floor Lathe**

- This kind of lathe has different sizes.
- The swing has a length that ranges between 10 and 25 inches.
- The power of this lathe ranges between ½hp and 3hp.
- This lathe can turn a wide variety of projects.

5. Center or Engine Lathe

- It has components like the lathe bed, the saddle, tailstock, and headstock.
- It is fixed to a point.
- Cutting tools can easily be fed into it either longitudinally or transversely.
- It is usually driven by a gear mechanism. The types of driven mechanisms include ones driven by belts, ones driven by motors, and the others driven by gear heads.
- It is used for grooving, knurling, threading, etc.

6. Speed Lathe

- This is also known as the wood lathe.
- It functions at very high speeds, within a range of 1200 to 3600 revolutions per minute.

- Here, the headstock spindle revolves at a high speed.
- This lathe has a headstock, a tailstock, but no feed mechanisms. You have to feed your cutting tool manually.
- This device can be used for spinning, centering, and polishing wood.

7. Capstan and Turret Lathe
- This lathe is used to produce pieces in large quantities.
- It is the adjusted version of the center lathe.
- Instead of a tailstock, it has a turret head that is in the shape of a hexagon.
- This device has three tool posts.
- It needs a lot of floor space to function.
- Beginners can easily handle this lathe.
- It is used for turning, facing, boring, and reaming.

8. Toolroom Lathe
- This device works at a speed of 2500 revolutions per minute and even more.
- It has a similar build to the center lathe.

- This lathe is perfect for works that require high levels of precision.

9. Special Purpose Lathe
- This lathe offers a few operations RHA the other lathe machines do not offer.
- The lathe can be used to produce identical items.
- The types of special lathes include special lathe, the wheel lathe, the duplicate or tracer lathe, etc.

10. Computerized Numerically Controlled Lathe
- This lathe is one of the most advanced ones available.
- It works with a great level of precision.
- You control your tools here with computerized codes.
- This lathe works best for massive production.

Chuck

Chucks are used to fasten woodblocks to the headstock of your lathe device while they are being turned. With a chuck, you can have a firm grip on one end of the wood while turning hollow grooves on the other side. An example of a project that uses the technique above is the eggcup project. The tailstock gets in the way most times and ends up not supporting the hollowed end. So, that's why chucks are necessary as they retain a strong grip on the wood being turned.

For turning bowls, the chuck holds on to the base of the bowl while you make a hollow in the insides. You could even turn out the exterior sides of the bowl at the same time.

Using chucks cancel out the need for screws and tailstock support. The kind of chuck you get depends on the kind of turning project you want to do. You will need large chucks for large projects, and for small projects, you will need small chucks. Another thing to consider is the size of your lathe. You wouldn't want to work with a large chuck on a mini lathe, would you?

Doing that would just wear out the bearings in the headstock quickly. So, ensure you check the spindle size of the headstock of your lathe before you get any chuck. One of the common sizes of headstocks available includes the 1¼" by 8".

The chuck you get could be multi-purpose scroll chucks or specific purpose chucks. The jaws of chucks are fixed to the chucks themselves by depressed machine screws. The jaws are also borne by the expansible and contractible jaw slides. Chucks have inner gears that make all the jaws move fluidly and simultaneously.

You can adjust your jaws by using the tool that comes with the chuck. Most times, the screws are either tightened or loosened with the aid of hex tools or chuck keys. You'd find two screw points with each at the opposite ends of the chuck.

Four-jawed chucks have four jaws that open and close alternatively to grip the project. The four-jawed self-centering scroll chuck with dovetail joints is still the one that is commonly used the most.

The Jacobs chuck has a drill in either the headstock or tailstock that helps make neat holes in wood.

Features you should look out for in your chuck

1. Dovetail joints. This feature strengthens the dovetail joints you made in woodblocks as they are structured in a way that locks in a shaped project. Ensure that the dovetail joints can expand and lock into various shapes at the bottom of the bowl.

2. Go for jaws that can be easily interchanged. This feature will be very essential for projects of different sizes.

3. T-bar mechanism. This mechanism constitutes gears that are confined within the chuck. They enable you to tighten their grip on the wood stock one-handedly with little or no effort at all.

4. Interchangeable threading. This feature will be very good if you get a new lathe as you will have to change the thread lines in the chuck to accommodate the spindle of the new lathe.

5. Quality steel. Good chucks are built with hardened metals like iron and the bodies are usually plated to make them resistant to wears, tears, and rusts.

6. Indexing holes. These holes allow you to screw the chuck in when performing projects that require drilling and routing.

Woodturning Tools

These tools include chisels, gouges, scrapers, parting tool, etc. They all work to bring out the outline of any project you are working on.

Types of woodturning tools

Spindle Roughing Gouge

- This tool is a hefty tool that can get rid of as much wood stock as you need while turning wood. The final cuttings may not look too neat, but then, it is effective in what it does.
- You can use this tool to turn a square or off-center piece round about its edges.
- It has a broad U-shaped flute that can quickly get rid of wood stock.

- You shouldn't use the spindle roughing gouge to work on faceplate projects as it can lead to the blade getting caught by the wood fibers.
- If you are going to cover many areas with this tool, you'd better use a gouge with $\frac{7}{8}$" size.

Spindle Gouge

- This tool is also known as the shaper.
- It helps you to carve out the outline of spindle work and for cutting out intricate details.
- You can use this tool to create beads of wooden pieces.
- Spindle gouges have a shallow flute.
- You can find this tool in a variety of dimensions
- They have tiny edges that are ground back for versatility.
- To do something very detailed and beautifully shaped, you could work with a gouge of $\frac{1}{2}$".

Skew Chisel

- Using this tool requires you to have a little bit of technical know-how.
- This tool is sharpened on both of its edges.
- On this tool, the cutting edge should be at an angle of thirty degrees to the edges.
- With this tool, you can cut both to the right and the left.
- The bevel's length must be equal to twice the thickness of the chisel wherever it is sharpened.
- The wheel should have a diameter of about six inches so that the bevel will be left quite hollow.
- This tool can be very good for smoothing out a plane surface.
- A skew chisel has a rounded top, and a bottom edge that is flat so that you could easily maneuver it.

- Ensure that the skew's cutting edge is always in contact with the wood at an angle of 45°. It must also be above the central lines of the wood stock so that you can easily move it from one end to the other.

Parting Tool

- This tool is usually sharpened at both of its edges.
- The difference between this tool and an ordinary chisel is that it has a thickness that varies between ⅝" and ¾". Even at its widest points, it can only go about ⅛", which falls at the center of its entire length.
- Its bevels must meet at the center or the widest point so that they are inclined at an angle of 50° to each other.
- This makes the final cuts in your projects.

- This helps you separate the final piece from the other irrelevant pieces when cutting between central points.
- Parting tools are very suitable for plunge cuts.

Bowl Gouge
- This tool has a deep flute.
- The Bowl gouge is beveled at its outer edges and ground in a way that the nose has a semi-circular shape.
- This tool is a fuse of the properties of a round nose chisel and an ordinary gouge.
- When using this tool, ensure that the bevel reaches its ends so that its cutting edges can extend to both sides. This technique will prevent the issue of abrupt corners.
- You can use this tool to carve out both the inner and outer parts of the bowl.
- To finish the inner parts of a bowl, you could use a bottom feeder bowl gouge.
- There are two shapes in which the bowl gouge flute exists. There's the 'U-shape' and the 'V-shape.' The 'U-shaped' gouge flute is used for

cutting out the interior parts of a bowl. The 'V-shaped' bowl gouge is versatile and can be used for finishing and roughening bowl projects.

Scraper

- This is a finishing tool that is used to smoothen the surface of a finished project.
- The round nose, square nose, spear point, right skew, left skew, etc., are all types of scraping tools.
- The scraping tool is mostly used in pattern and faceplate projects.
- Scrapers have only one sharp edge and a bevel that is two times the thickness of the chisel at its sharp edge.
- Scrapers quickly lose their sharp edges when they come in contact with the wood at right angles. For this reason, you must sharpen this tool as often as possible to get great results.
- To work with this tool, you can whizz through the surface of the wood instead of cutting through it again.

- This tool is used to get rid of marks left by bowl gouges on the woodblock. This particular technique makes the scraper tool very useful for beginners as they can easily get rid of any error they make.
- When working with this tool, direct it at a downward angle. You could also hold it at an angle of 30° from the horizontal tool rest.
- A nose scraper which is also known as a bowl scraper is used to get rid of the marks within the bowl.
- A square nose scraper helps to get rid of marks fixed to the outer part of the bowls, boxes, and flat surfaces.

Other woodturning tools that will cone very handy in your projects are:

1. Turning tools: They are structured to cut through a wooden block to obtain the final project. Turning tools will help to increase the quality of the wooden surface.

2. Boring bar: This tool works to make a previously drilled hole bigger. No matter the diameter of the hole, the boring bar works to extend it to something that will take in other components of the lathe easily.

3. Chamfering tool: Chamfers are the edges that exist between the faces of wooden joints.

Chamfers have the look of bevels. The chamfering tool works to create bevels in wood. To smoothen the sharp and dangerous edges of your project, you could use the chamfering tool.

4. Knurling tool: This tool helps to create certain designs, knurls, and patterns on wood by pressing the outlines to the round sections of the wood.

5. Thread cutting tool: This tool is used to cut through the thread in the lathe machine. When the cutting procedure is done outside the lathe, the thread is usually fixed between two central points. However, if it is done externally, the cutting tool scrapes across the wood's length in straight lines.

6. Facing tool: This tool is used to cut out flat surfaces that are perpendicular to the rotational axis of the lathe. To go through with this procedure, the cutting tool is mounted upon a tool holder and is fed at a ninety-degree angle to the lathe's rotational axis.

7. Grooving tool: This tool is structured so that it bears several tips with each tip of the size needed for a particular project.

Setting Up a Woodturning Workshop

After you get your wood lathe, you have to consider the processes involved in installing and setting up the device. Unfortunately, several people do not know how crucial this step is to get maximum results. First, you might need to get a working space. A rented office or a free room in your house will do just fine, but then, the most important thing is the space you have to work with. Bluntly speaking, you will need a lot of space to set up a lathe device. Besides, you will be working with other tools apart from the lathe device, which equally takes up space. A few of those things include the band saw, the bench grinders, dividers, calipers, cutting tools, and so on. Some of these devices and tools demand that they be mounted on benches and so, you can only imagine how much space that will require.

Other points to note when setting up your workshop are given below.

- Ensure there is a lot of space between the benches bearing all the devices and the walls. This way, if you ever have to work with extremely long or broad materials, you wouldn't have any issue.

- The area of space you should set aside for woodturning should be nothing less than a measure of seventy-five square feet. The highest area of space to work with should measure about one hundred and twenty-five feet that should store wood logs.

- The size of the working space you will need is determined by the number of fixed equipment you work with for your operations. Each machine should be placed at a distance of 3 feet apart. If the space you are working with is too limited for this degree of freedom, you could fix your devices to bases with wheels. Be careful that your machines do not clutter the whole space. There has to be space for you to move freely without having to pause to get rid of the obstruction.

- The dust collection system is another feature you must include in your workshop. While turning your wood, there's certainly going to be heaps of wood shavings and sawdust. Once the air picks up these particles and your breathing space gets saturated with them, you could be at risk of respiratory diseases and lung ailments. A modern dust collection system is made of central ducts and pipes and a flexible tubing system that leads to a general dust collector.

- Before you settle on any kind of duct system, it would be best to consider your working space's size and the measurements of the duct pipes you want to use. Air filtration units are also other effective ways of getting rid of wood dust.

- The major workbench should be structured in a way that you can easily work with the lathe while sitting or standing. It'd be even more preferable if you made it an adjustable workbench.

- Ensure that your workspace is flooded with natural light (sunlight) or bright artificial lights. Work in areas with a lot of windows and openings to allow more light in. You could also paint the ceilings and the walls in white or off-white color so that there can be a maximum reflection of light within the room. For artificial lights, know that fluorescent bulbs are much brighter than incandescent lightings. It is also cheaper and easier to work with

- Ensure that your workshop has access to a lot of lighting and stable electricity. In case you are working with a lot of machines, you could also get a medium-sized electrical panel for your shop. It ensures that you get a stable electricity supply across your workshop.

- Ensure that the counter is about seven inches above the lathe. The center of the shaft's distance from the center of the spindle should not be more than six inches.

- The countershaft should be in a direction parallel to the line shaft. When the countershaft is in position, the bob should be hung from the counter shaft's cone to the spindle cone.

- The lathe device must be set in a way that the belt moves between the two cone pulleys. The lathe must be on an axis that runs parallel to the countershaft. However, the lathe does not need to be right under the counter shelf as the belt usually works at an angle to the horizontal planes.

Woodturning Safety Tips and Best Practices

1. Protect your eyes. A lathe machine can roll at very insane speeds and as you cut through the woodblock mounted on it, the scrapings travel in a direction that is at a tangent to the direction of the rolling stock. This angle means that chips of wood can easily hit you or scratch your cornea if you aren't too careful. To prevent that, wear safety googles. Common eyeglasses will not even do the trick as it doesn't cover every part of your eye. It could just sit lazily on the bridge of your nose. Wearing a full face shield is another thing you should consider.

Wearing face shields equipped with sound protectors and helmets with air filtration units can also be very useful. These filtration units see to it that you have supplied to your nose an endless channel of filtered air. If wood dust ever finds its way to your eyes, it could irritate the conjunctiva, water, or redness of the eye. If we considered the adverse effects the wood dust could have on your air passages, one could have issues like runny noses, sneezing, or even asthma attacks.

2. If you are allergic to a particular kind of wood, do not cut through it or use it for any of your turning projects. For example, wood blocks with fungal matter can be very dangerous if you inhale the dust created when you either turn the wood or smoothen the surface with sandpaper.

3. Take time to rest in between your projects.

4. Make sure your working space is not cluttered with extension cords. You wouldn't want to trip

because of them or suffer a hazard caused by an overloaded circuit. If you have to run the cords haphazardly, ensure that you have them taped to the floor.

5. Make sure you do not wear loose clothing or jewelry while working on the lathe machine. You could pack your hair up into a bun or tuck it inside a cap.

6. If you are working with a bench lathe, ensure that it is properly bolted to the tabletop, and if it is a floor lathe, see that it is fixed tightly to it too.

7. Turn the hand brake as often as possible before starting your turning work to ensure that the wood stock does not make contact with the tool rest or any other lose component of the lathe.

8. Ensure that the tool rest points towards the center of the wood stock so that it would spin smoothly when you turn on the lathe.

9. Each kind of project you work on has a speed that the lathe must work with. Projects with large diameter turnings require the lathe machine to spin at low speeds. You should also ensure that you start with the lowest speeds possible. You can gradually increase the speed as you continue. If you work at high speed, the table might vibrate too much, which is not good for the lathe machine's headstock.

10. Work with sharp tools. Tools with blunt edges will make irregular and rough cuts. Besides, if you use sharp cutting tools, you wouldn't have to exert much pressure on the tool before cutting through the wood.

11. When you are working, see that you stand at the right stance that makes you comfortable. The wrong stance can make your neck and back muscles feel strained. And from there, you could end up getting tired faster than you would want.

Stand in a direction parallel to the lathe and keep your feet at shoulder-width.

12. While you work on your project, keep one hand on the tool rest and the other hand at the end of the tool, just close to your hip. All you need to do is to move your body back and forth as you cut.

13. Ensure that you properly dispose of the materials you use to finish as they could get burnt if you aren't too careful.

14. Before you lay hands on any lathe device, read the manufacturer's manual, and see that you understand every line in it. Comply with every safety instruction written in the manual too to prevent unnecessary injuries. Even after reading a manual, ensure that you seek advice and counseling from those who are skilled with the device before trying it out.

15. Before powering your lathe, check for issues like poor configurations or any other binding that could cause an issue if not tightened.

16. While working, avoid distractions like pets and kids.

17. Do not work with your lathe device if you are tired, sick, or under the influence of alcohol or drugs.

18. Before adjusting the tool rest of your lathe device, wait for the lathe to stop running completely. Do not try to alter anything related to the tool rest while the lathe is powered. You also shouldn't try to use your hands to stop a wooden stock from rolling.

19. Before you begin work with a lathe device, make sure the wood stock is firmly mounted between the headstock's drive center and the tailstock's

live center. Also, ensure that the project is firmly held by the four-jawed chuck. To be extra careful, you could use both the chuck and the tailstock of the lathe device to hold on firmly to your project.

20. Before you start your lathe device, spin the woodblock with your hand to ensure that any component on the lathe bed does not stop its motion. You should also ensure that the handles of the lathe device are locked tightly in place.

21. Make sure all the safety features have been activated before you start working with your lathe. If there are any unnecessary work items on the lathe bed, take them away before you begin any project.

22. Inspect the woodblock for cracks, splits, or other defects that could tamper with the quality of your project. These cracks can cause the project to crumble or break out of the lathe's hold. Even as

you turn the woodblock, pause intermittently to check the thinning block for any signs of defect.

23. Do not leave the lathe running when you aren't working with it.

24. Do not use the wrong tools for any project you work on as it could lead to serious disasters. For example, you should never use a spindle roughing gouge to turn a bowl. They don't have the strength to handle face-turning and may end up breaking along the process.

25. When working with a lathe device, remain composed and steady. Do not exert too much pressure while doing any project. Just stay calm and collected.

26. While you turn a piece of wood, make sure you keep your hands at the back of the tool rest. If any of your fingers get to tuck in the junction between

your tool rest and turning stock, you might end up being severely injured.

27. To ensure you have total control of your turning tools, use both of your hands. One could regulate the cutting edge and the other should grip the handle.

28. Before sanding your project on the lathe, make sure you move the tool rest and its holder (the banjo) out of the way. Without shifting those components away, you might end up twisting your wrist at its joint.

29. Do not use clothes to rub in polish or finish on the wood stock while it is mounted on rotating wood stock. If the cloth gets caught by a fiber of the wood that hasn't blended with the regular surface, it could direct your hand towards the spin and inflict on you a very terrible injury.

Sharpening Woodturning Tools

When your turning tools are well sharpened, you would be able to make cleaner cuts on your wood stock. For this purpose, getting a good grinding system for your projects might just be the best thing to do.

Tools used for sharpening turning tools

1. Bench grinder.
2. Grinder wheels.
3. Grinding jigs.
4. Skew and attachment, e.g., the Vari Grind attachment.
5. Turning tools.
6. Diamond wheel dresser.
7. Protractor.
8. Square gauge.
9. Angle gauge.

There are two types of grinding systems. They are the dry and wet grinding systems. The wet system is an effective method in that it involves getting the tool sharpened in a tank of water. It also yields a sharper edge than the one a dry system will yield. Other issues like heat generation and reduction in the temperature generated by friction are also avoided while using this system.

However, dry grinding systems are more convenient and less stressful to use. When working with a dry grinding system, the first thing you should consider is whether or not the grinder is to be mounted on a bench or fixed to the floor. In whatever option you choose, make sure that the motor powering the device has about ½hp rating. The wheels should also have a diameter of about eight inches.

Grinding wheels

Grinding wheels exist with various grits. The ones with an 80-grit system are usually used for shaking wood while the ones with a 120-grit system are used for finishing your projects. If you want your finishes to be neat enough, you should ensure that your grinding wheels are well balanced. It will also help the wheels to stand the test of time and cancel the harmful risk of vibration across the bench or any other working surface. These vibrations work to destroy the bearings and compartments in your grinder. To balance the wheels, follow the manufacturer's instructions.

Wheel dressers.

Wheel dressers help improve your grinding wheels' functionality by evacuating dust, metallic particles, and any other debris that sticks to them. If your grinding wheels are kept clean, you would be able to make cleaner cuts on your tools.

Your grinding wheel must assume a concave shape and not a flat one as it will help you sharpen your tools more effectively without having their edges fired by the action of friction. For sharpening your tools to the maximum point, you should make use of tools like diamond dressers. There's a kind of diamond dresser that cleans your wheel dresser with a single point diamond held straight by an adjustable arm. This diamond crust is what sounds across the wheel's surface to create a clean and flat surface.

Apart from the single point diamond dresser, you could also work with a diamond jig. This one has several chips of diamond packed into the surface of the dresser.

Grinding Jig.

Grinding systems work will tool like gouges, scrapers, skews, and other carving tools. When you sharpen them, they have to be at an angle to the wheel of the grinder so that you can get the best results. You should also ensure that you get a grinding wheel that can form several angles with reduced wear and tear issues. It is a very important factor for your first woodturning projects.

To know if your tool is sharpened or not, you can use the principle of reflection. A sharp tool will have no light reflecting off its surface or edges. However, if the light is reflected from its edges, you need to sharpen the tool. To get good results when you use a grinding wheel for the first time, ensure that you set the wheels at the same angle at which the manufacturer set them when the tool was sharpened. You can also use a protractor or square to check for the angle of the tools. You can later alter the angle at which you sharpen your tools as you later proceed with your grinding projects. Sometimes, a few projects may require the cutting tools to be at different angles.

How to sharpen a parting tool

- For a parting tool, you should work at an angle of twenty-five degrees.
- The platform has to be perpendicular to the grinding wheel.

- Place the parting tool flatly on the platform and press the tool lightly against grinding wheels to sharpen the tools.

How to sharpen a roughing gouge

- When sharpening a roughing gouge, you should use the same kind of bevel that the manufacturer worked with. The angle you should work with when sharpening your roughing gouge is 45°.
- Use a marker to mark the roughing gouge's bevel.
- Align the bevel with the grinding wheel.
- Rotate the wheel manually and lightly press the gouge to the grinding wheel to get rid of the mark made by the marker.
- Observe the bevel of the gouge to see the point where the mark was cut off. If the wheel cuts off the mark at the bottom of the bevel, move the jig slightly out to get regular contact with the total level. However, if the mark was cut off at the top of the tool, slightly push in the jig to get the bevels in line with the wheel.
- After you've got the right angle, grind the bevel's total length with a side-to-side motion.

- The corners of a roughing gouge usually grind more slowly than the middle of the tool would, so work to grind against the edges for a longer period to see that the square edges are retained.

How to grind a spindle gouge or a bowl gouge

- For a spindle gouge, you should work at an angle of 35°, while for a bowl gouge, you should work at an angle within the range of 50° and 55°. These angles are the only different things you should observe while sharping the tools.
- Mark the level of the spindle gouge with chalk and fix the gouge into the jig's pocket.
- Rub the bevel lightly on the wheel and adjust the shift of the jig either in or out depending on how the mark points are wiped off.
- Grind the gouge from one side to the other, making sure you cover the bevel's entire length until the tool is well sharpened. You could also grind both the spindle gouge and the bowl gouge to the side
- A spindle gouge is ground with a side grind or a fingernail profile. For the bottom, use the fingernail profile at an angle of 35°. Fingernail

control is easier to control and more comfortable for you to work with. There will also be fewer chances of the gouge sinking into the wood fibers with this method. You can also grind the edges of the bowl edges with a fingernail grind.

- For a side grind, use the Ellsworth grind, an Irish grind that involves sweeping and rolling motions on the jig. You would also need attachments like wolverine Vari-grind attachment. This tool will help you produce regular sharp bevels on your turning tools while you carve out the side grind for the spindle work.

- Fix the bowl gouge into the attached tool and adjust the grinding jig's pocket until the bevel rubs against the grinding wheel lightly.

- Power on the grinding machine and ensure that the attached tool is firmly resting against the jig's back pocket. Move the gouge from one side to the other in a sweeping motion and see that the pressure you exert is directed forward at all times.

How to grind the skew chisel

- This process is done at an angle of 60°.

- If you used a skew attachment tool with the sharpening mechanism, you'd be able to create a bevel with a flat and consistent surface.
- This jig's design helps to eradicate the issue of hollow grinds that are usually tied to sharpening a skew on a grinding wheel.
- Use a marker to mark the sides of the skew as with the roughing gouge.
- Fix the skew into the left pocket of the attached tool with the short point pointing towards the left.
- Line up the bevel with the skew and the grinding wheel.
- Move the skew back and forth while shifting your hands slightly from side to side. Once you are done with one side, turn the skew around and fix it inside the right pocket with the short point pointing to the right. Do this procedure again.
- The skew's bevel should be flat and continuous. Ensure that it doesn't turn out like a multi-faced edge.

How to sharpen a scraping tool

- This process should be done at an angle of 80°.

- Power the grinder on and move the scraper across the sides in a sweeping motion to sharpen the edges of the scraper.

Sanding Your Woodturning Projects

Sanding your turned projects is essential as it helps you get rid of a mark left by a tool and smoothen a surface or edge. This technique is the first thing you do when you start the finishing works on your projects. There are two methods you could use to sand your projects. There is the power sanding that you can use for faceplate projects and the hand sanding technique which you use for spindle projects.

Some of the sandpapers you can use for smoothening your turning projects include silicon carbide, aluminum oxide, garnet sandpaper, etc. These sanding papers have two grades. One is the commercial-grade and the other is the industrial grade.

The industrial-grade sandpaper can withstand a lot of pressure and harsh conditions from industries' work. This type of sandpaper needs heavy backing material and some glue or resin usually glues the abrasive. The other kind of sandpaper, the commercial one, is one you can get easily at stores. It requires light backing materials that are bonded to the abrasive by glue.

Power sanding

Power sanding is a technique employed for faceplate turning on objects with large surfaces. This technique makes the process of sanding a lot easier than the manual one. Angle sanders have heads that are joined with one another and can allow the head of the sanding pad to be used at several angles. This pad is moved about the surface of your project by spinning processes of the device. If you sand closer to a bowl project's outer edges, the sanding machine will work at an even higher speed. As you work your way towards the center, the speed of the machine reduces.

You could also power-sand your projects by fixing your sanding pads into the mouth of a hand drill. Hand drills worked with a turning lathe can also work to speed things up. Since the drill spins in an opposite direction to that of the lathe, the surface of your project gets smooth in no time. The only issue with this technique is that it causes the cracking of your project due to the effect of the heat generated. In the absence of a hand drill, you could work with a flexible shaft inserted into the mouth of your drill press. This technique is even more comfortable as it is lighter to work with than a hand drill.

Tools required for Power sanding are

- Angle sander and flexible shaft.
- Different kinds of sanding materials, each with grit that ranges between 60 and 800.
- Sanding pads

Hand sanding

This technique is rather manual as it involves you gripping the sandpaper and then, running it across the body of your project as it spins on a lathe device. For this stage, you could make use of sandpapers with wavy discs that have finger-like edges that move fluidly to help you get rid of swirl lines and sharp edges on the insides of your turned projects. The discs are also useful in bowl turning projects to get rid of marks left by circular sanding pads. They blend with the contour of the bowl and then, you can end up with a smooth surface.

Sandpapers like Abranetexists come in in several grits and as you sand your project, the grits don't get clumped up with wood dust particles. The dust can be wiped off with compressed air. You can also work with sanding materials that have their backing material made from foam.

Finishing Your Woodturning Projects

Finishing your project is the last thing you will need to do to end the hour-long turning work. However, this step also requires a high leave of meticulousness as it can easily make or mar your work. Before you choose any finish, think of how and where your product is going to be used. There are finishes for decorative pieces and there are less harmful finishes for kitchen wares. There is also the consideration of how easy it is to apply the finish. Do you like it in the form of aerosols or liquids? Do you want to apply it in sprays or by using a towel?

The appearance of your project is also another important factor. Your projects could have a glossy look or have the look of satin. If your project is something that will be fondled often, look for a finish that is resistant to scratches. You could even sell your projects faster by working with finishes that have nice textures.

Preparing the surface of your project for finishing

Before applying a finish to your project, ensure that marring outlines like tool marks, sanding scratches, end grain tear-out, or any other defects are cleared off the surface of the objects to be finished. The finish you apply on a project usually brings out the wood grains, and even the smallest hints of errors become evident at once. Fixing a bad finish will involve you sanding the surface over again and that can be very stressful. Before you apply a finish to your project, ensure that you have sanded the surface with grits up to 800. To remove the minuscule sanding dust particles, you will need a lint-free cloth. Doing this technique will give you the best finish possible.

How to apply the various types of finish

For kitchen wares, you will need the following finishing equipment.

- A salad bowl finish.
- Lint-free cloth.
- Different grits of sandpaper.

A salad bowl finish is a non-toxic finish that is safe for kitchenware. When dry, this finish has a dry and tough film that poses no harm to your food items. Once you coat your project with this finish, wait for about 3 days for it to dry as then, it will no longer contain contamination particles.

Use a lint-free cloth to rub the finish lightly on the surface of your project. You can add more layers if you aren't satisfied. When you are done, wipe off the excess finish with that same lint-free cloth. It is often essential that you dry the project in between each layer of finish for about six hours. After each layer, sand the surface before you coat it again with another layer of finish. The salad bowl finish has a brilliant sheen and is very resistant to scratches.

How to apply Tung oil

You'll need the following to apply this finish;

- Tung oil.
- Mineral Spirits.
- 400-grit sandpaper or a 4000 grit sanding pad.
- A brush or a lint-free cloth.

Tung oil is one of the most durable finishes you could ever use for your projects. It is also suitable for kitchenware as it does not contain harmful compounds or ingredients. The Tung oil finish is usually consistent and hard enough to resist scratches. It is resistant to water, stains, scratches, and even heat. If you work with the pure form of Tung oil, you might have to thin the layers over and over again with mineral spirits. The mixture of the spirits with the Tung oil will create a chance for the finish to penetrate deep inside the project.

To apply this finish, use either a brush or a lint-free cloth to rub the surface of the project. Before you remove the excess, wait for the wood's fibers to absorb the oil first. In between each cost, wait for about twenty-four hours, then use sandpaper to smoothen the surfaces of the project. For bowls with natural edges, apply the finish across the edges to allow the oil to penetrate the wood deeply.

How to apply a spray lacquer

Things needed to apply a spray lacquer on your project.

- Sanding sealant.
- Spray lacquer.
- 400-grit sanding paper or 0000-steel wool.

Before you use a spray lacquer, you have to ensure that the surface of your project is entirely devoid of dust or dirt. You should also ensure that you spray the lacquer in a place with cross-ventilation.

Before you work with spray lacquer, you should also see to it that you apply a coat of sanding sealant to the surface of your project first. This sealant fills your project's small pores and allows the fibers to rise to their regular surface. When you sand this layer, you can be sure of a very smooth surface.

Apply coats of the spray lacquer at right angles to each other to get a strong, clear, and tough layer for the final coat of spray lacquer. After each coat, sand the surface of your project with 4000-grit sandpaper or the 0000-steel wool. For the final spray of lacquer, place your hand at a distance of 12meters from the project then move it back and forth. Do not keep your hand in one position for long to ensure that you get a regular surface. Build the finish thinly before you proceed to thicker layers. Do not try to finish the whole process in a single spray. All you will end up with are drips of running fluid across your project, which can be very bad.

Chapter 5

Woodturning Project Ideas

Shoehorn

Supplies

- Roughing gouge.
- Skew chisel or spindle master.
- Parting tool.
- Calipers.
- Wood stock—1½″ by 1½″ by 12″.
- Sanding paper.
- A shoehorn kit.
- 23/64″ drill bit.
- CA glue.
- Any finish of your choice.
- A lathe device with its speed set within the range of 500 to 2000 revolutions per minute.

Procedure

1. Layout all the pieces of equipment you will be working with, including the square wood stock with a length of about twelve inches.

2. Just at the ends of the woodblock, draw lines from each corner in an 'X' form and then mark the center where the lines intersect. Drive the drive spur through the center with a mallet.

3. Mount the wood stock between the center of the two spindle stocks.

4. Scrape through the square wooden stock with a roughing gouge until it is reduced to something with a cylindrical shape. You could also use a tool with a changeable tip like the new edge round scraper.

5. Use a spindle master or skew chisel to smoothen the now cylindrical surface. You would notice that the center of the cylinder releases very clean wood shavings.

6. With a parting tool, cut across the ends of the spindle, a cut of about ⅞".

7. The shoehorn should be about 7" in length.

8. To ensure that the cuts have the same diameter, use calipers to measure them.

9. Use a skew chisel to reduce the cylinder to a cut, as shown in the image below.

Measure the inner diameter of the cap's end with calipers.

10. With that same measurement, reduce one end of the cylinder to a size that matches the inner diameter.
11. At the other end of the cylindrical stock, create some beads, lines, or any other embellishing of your choice.

12. With a skew chisel, rub the bevel against the wood and then, roll it towards the right. The skew chisel must have its flat edge facing you. You should also ensure that the bevel is in contact with the cylindrical stock all through. Do the same thing for the rest of the beads.
13. If you can't carve out the beads perfectly, you could use sandpaper to regularise the edges.

14. Sand the rest of the cylindrical stock. Start from a sanding paper of 100 grits and continue until you get to one with 800 grits. To get rid of micro-scratches, use sanding pads.

15. Finish the project with any finish of your choice.
16. Use a parting tool to reduce the ends of the cylindrical stock a little. Make sure that you still leave a wood scrap that the headstock can hold on to.
17. While one hand holds the parting tool, use the other hand to catch the piece as you pull it away from the tailstock.

18. Fix the back end of the cylindrical stock into a four-jawed chuck. Then, use a 23/64" drill bit to

bore a hole into the opposite end of the horn end of the shoehorn.

19. To remove the nub at the end of the spindle, use a spindle gouge.

20. Glue the brass end to the shoehorn using a CA glue.
21. You are done!

Spindle Turning Pen

Supplies

- Roughing gouge.
- Spindle master.
- Drill center.
- Barrel trimmer.

- Pen insertion tool.
- Pen mandrel.
- Pen press.
- Any pen kit of your choice.
- CA glue and accelerator.
- Pen blank.
- Wood Turner's finish.
- Sanding pads.
- A Lathe running at a speed set between 1000 and 2500 revolutions per minute.

Procedure

1. Unbox the tools in the kit and then, follow the guide that comes with the kit to know how you'll turn the project.
2. To cut the pen's wooden stock, guide your cutting with a pen tube.
3. For the tubes to stick well to the inner parts of the pen blank, roughen the surface by rubbing it with a piece of sandpaper.
4. Use a drill centering tool to drill through the pen blank with the right sized drill bit for the kind of pen kit you chose.

5. Glue the pen tubes to the wooden penstock with a medium grade CA glue. To prevent the glue from staining your fingers, use a tool to spread it across the wood's surface.

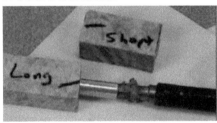

6. To remove the excess glue inside the tube, use a barrel trimming tool. The pen must be placed squarely to the pen blank.
7. Place the mandrel into the headstock of your lathe device. Then, position the pen blanks onto the mandrel in the right setting. For the right setting, note the marks on the pen blank.

8. Screw the locking but into the mandrel and make sure it is very tight. However, you shouldn't make the lock too tight to prevent damage to the mandrel. The pen might also not turn in symmetrical axes. There also shouldn't be too much pressure on the mandrel from the tailstock

9. Let the gouge touch the pen blank lightly and then, move it back and forth to make the pen blank round. For this technique, use a roughing gouge and a bevel.
10. To shape the pen blank, use a skew chisel. You can also use a Spindle master if you aren't too good with the skew chisel. The pen blank should be slightly higher than the bushings.
11. The sanding grit you start with should depend on the pen blank having tool marks or scratches. If you don't have too many scratches on the project from the skew chisel you used, you can start with 220-grit sandpaper.

12. Sand the surface of the project with sandpaper of grits as high as 800. Then after that, use sanding pads. The pads will get rid of the micro scratches.

13. With a towel, rub the surface of the project with any finish of your choice while it is being rotated with a lathe.

14. Increase the speed of the lathe and use a piece of cloth to apply pressure on the finish's surface. This technique will help you to lock in the finish onto the project.

15. The next thing to do is to apply a wood turner's finish to the first layer of dried finish with a paper towel.

16. Align the finished pen pieces according to the instructions given for the pen's assembly on the kit.
17. Use a pen press to press the front end coupler and the end cap into the lower portion of the barrel as instructed on the pen kit.
18. You are done!

Faceplate Turning a Bowl

Supplies

- ½" bowl gouge with a fingernail profile.
- A curved scraper and a round nose scraper.
- Four-jawed chucks and mini jaws.
- Faceplate and 1¼" square drive screws.
- Double-end calipers.
- Dividers or compass.
- Sanding pads.
- Sanding paper in different grits.
- Maple wood with a diameter of 8 inches and a thickness of 4 inches.
- A lathe device with the speed set between 500 and 1500 revolutions per minute.
- Salad bowl finish

Procedure

1. Find the center of the bowl blank and then mount the faceplate on it using a 1¼" square drive screw.
2. Fix the faceplate to the headstock and use the tailstock as a support for the bowl blank. Roll the hand brake to ensure that the blank does not hit

the tool rest. The lathe must move at a minimum speed of 500 revolutions per minute.

3. Use a bowl gouge to work through the headstock to the tailstock with small bites while seeing to it that the blank is well balanced.

4. Make the face of the blank leveled and then make a spigot for the four-jawed chuck.

5. Start at the edge of the blank and cut from the back to the front swiftly to prevent getting a surface with a lot of irregularities.

6. Use a pair of dividers to mark the right width for a four-jawed chuck. You also have to ensure that the divider's right side doesn't touch the spinning bowl.

7. Use a bowl gouge to reduce the diameter of the spigot so that it can fit into the chuck.

8. If you are okay with the shape of the bowl, sand the blank with a power sander to get rid of the tool marks and scratches. If you still see more marks after using the power sander, you can use sandpaper with a rough grit to get rid of them.

9. For the final sanding, use sanding pads that work to get rid of the micro scratches.

10. Turn the bowl around and then insert it inside the four-jawed chuck.
11. Working your way from the edge of the bowl to the center, ensure that the bevel is parallel to the bowl's surface. This is where you will want to fix the bowl's thickness.
12. Power off the lathe machine and position the gouge so that you can make cuts towards the center of the bowl.
13. To continue cutting, make sure the bevel's contact with the wood is even till it gets to the center of the bowl.
14. Check the thickness of the walls of the bowl at this point with calipers to ensure that you work with a certain degree of thickness. Try to get rid of one inch of the wall's material bit by bit so that the wood's fibers are held firmly by the layer below them. If you removed too many fibers, it might get difficult for you to keep the interiors regular.
15. Place any flat edge across the face of the bowl and then, use a ruler to measure the bowl's depth.
16. Move the flat edge to the top of the bowl to know how much material you need to get rid of.

17. Use a round nose scraper to get rid of the nub that is left at the bottom of the bowl. The bottom must be flat and free from ridges. For any scraper, make sure the tip is a little bit away from the bowl's centerline.
18. Use a power sander to smoothen the insides of the bowl. Make sure you keep the dust collection system close as you work.
19. Use wavy sanding discs because they work better on the insides of the bowl and leave no scratch lines in the process.
20. Use sanding pads to smoothen the bowl's insides and get rid of the micro scratches.
21. See that the bowl is properly aligned to the four-jawed chuck.
22. Use the mini jumbo jaw to secure the bowl so that you can easily turn the bottom of the bowl.
23. From the bottom, remove the spigot by taking small bites with the aid of a small bowl gouge.
24. Across the bottom of the bowl, place a straight edge and see that it has a slightly concave surface.
25. You can embellish the bottom of the bowl with lines and small coves.
26. Make sure to spin your project as you work.

27. Use the salad bowl finish to coat the surfaces.

28. Once the finish dries up, use 4000-grit sandpaper to sand the bowl before applying another salad bowl coat.

29. You are done.

Faceplate Turning an Ornamental Birdhouse

Supplies

- Any wood of bright color—1½″ by 1½″ by 2½″
- Roughing gouge.
- Skew chisel or Spindle master.
- Spindle gouge.
- Parting tool.

- Calipers.
- ½" and 1¼" of Forstner bits.
- ⅛" drill bit.
- Sandpaper of different grits.
- Sanding pads.
- Wood turner's finish.
- Wood stains—blood red, blue, yellow.
- Black acrylic paint.
- Finishing oil.
- CA glue of medium viscosity.
- A lathe device that works at a speed that ranges between 1000 and 2000 revolutions per minute.

Procedure

1. Mark the center of your wooden blank after drawing the lines from each corner of the box.
2. Use a drilling tool with a Forstner bit to bore a hole through the intersection.
3. Get a chuck of 1¼ inch diameter set in place. Then, mount a 2" by 2" by 6" woodblock on a four-jawed chuck.
4. Use a roughing gouge to carve out the square stock before working with the skew chisel.

5. Ensure that the chuck has a diameter of about 1¼" diameter or else it won't fit into the hole you drilled into the woodblock.

6. Place the wood blank on the chuck.

7. Use a roughing gouge to reduce the square stock to a round cylinder. You should only stop reducing the blank when you get a thickness that is about 1/32" thick.

8. Use a skew chisel to get a smooth finish.

9. Use a ⅛" parting tool to square the two ends of the woodblock. After that, sand the surface of the project with sandpaper.

10. From the top of the ornament, measure ⅜" and then, bore an opening for the point where the bird sits on the project. Then, measure a hole with a ¼" diameter for the perch. To support the drill bits, bore holes on the top of the jam chuck.

11. Use the four-jawed chuck to hold another piece of the maple wood to form the ornament's bottom. Make sure the ornament is only 1⅛" wide. You'd notice that this dimension is larger than the external diameter readings.

12. Carve out the base of the project into a round bottom with a width of 1". Reduce the width of

the base until it is just right at the base of the ornament's body. Sand both pieces to get a tight fit, but do not glue them together.

13. Use a small gouge to remove the wood on the inside of the ornament's base to reduce its weight. You needn't make perfect cuts here since it will be glued to the ornament's body. Follow the shape of the base and part it using a small parting tool.

14. With gloves covering your hands and fingers, prepare the wood stain by mixing the yellow and blue stains to get a color similar to green. To increase or decrease the intensity of any color, you can choose to use less or more of either of the component colors.

15. Turn the lathe at a speed of 1200rpm and then use a lint-free cloth to apply the green stain to the body of the ornament.

16. Once you are done with that, apply any finish of your choice.

17. With the CA glue you got earlier, glue the base of the ornament's green body and then fix it on top of the jam chuck.

18. Fix a ⅛″ drill bit to a Jacobs Chuck and then place the chuck in the tailstock.
19. Use the chuck to bore a hole of ⅛″ at the bottom of the ornament's base.
20. You can now stain the bottom of the ornament. Ensure that the mortise you create fits into the confines of the base before parting it with a parting tool.
21. Reduce a different piece of wood stock for the roof of the ornament to something of a diameter of two inches. Use a single gouge to shape the birdhouse's roof. Then, use the parting tool to make a small mortise under the roof for the body of the ornament.
22. Cut out the roof's inner parts with a small bowl gouge and then make light cuts to peel off wood from the inside. This technique will make the project lighter. Ensure that you do not remove too much wood, though.
23. Use a spindle gouge to continue shaping the wood. Bring the tailstock to the roof, sand it, and then separate the roof section from the lathe device.

24. Place the roof piece on a jam chuck and then use a very small numbered drill to make a hole at the top of the roof.
25. Stain the roof with a blood-red color.
26. With a paper towel, rub in any finish of your choice.
27. Use CA glue to fix the drill bit to the roof. Leave the glue to dry for a few minutes.
28. For the perch, glue a small piece of wood with a diameter of ½ inch and a length of 2 inches to a piece of scrap wood. Sand, stain, and finish the perch the way you want it to be.
29. Use the black acrylic paint to darken the inside of the ornament to give the impression that it has a lot of space in it. Glue the perch in the perch hole, which is the final base to the roof of the main ornament.
30. You are done!

Faceplate Turning a Natural Edge Bowl

Supplies

- A bowl gouge with a fingernail profile.
- A four-jawed chuck and worm screw.
- A curved scraper.
- A round nose scraper.
- Double-ended calipers.
- Any wood of your choice—6" diameter and 4" thickness.

- Sanding pads and sandpapers of different grit sizes.
- Turner's two-way tape.
- Tung Oil
- A lathe device rotating between 500 to 200 revolutions per minute.
- Two pieces of a 2" foam insulation.
- Any thin rubber-type material.

Procedure

1. Locate the center of your wood blank with the help of a template. Use an awl to drill through the center.
2. Once you get the center points, fix the blank between the drive spur and the tailstock. Take note of where the tool rest is supposed to be as it will help you locate the areas with the irregularities on the blank.
3. Use your hand to rotate the blank again until one of the blank's edges gets close to the edge of the tool rest.
4. Rotate the blank through an angle of 180° so you can observe how close the edge of the blank is to the tool rest. Both sides should have the same

distances from the tool rest. If one side isn't at the same distance, adjust the blank by moving its back in the tailstock until the distances are equal.

5. Adjust the height of the tool rest and rotate the hand brake so that the bowl blank does not touch the tool rest. For this procedure, set your lathe device to the slowest speed. Since the blank is not round yet, the device could vibrate a lot. That's normal.

6. Shape the blank by cutting off the body in small bites.

7. Make a final finishing cut on the outer surface of the bowl. Then, use a power sander to sand the outer surfaces. Start with 100-grit sandpaper and use sanding pads later on to get rid of the micro scratches.

8. Fix the gouge close to the tool rest. The bevel of the gouge should be parallel to the inside of the bowl each time you cut. Continue to push the gouge into the bowl while seeing that the bowl supports the bevel of the gouge.

9. Deal with the thickness of the walls at this point.

10. When you get to the middle of the bowl, ensure that the gouge's bevel is still in contact with the bottom of the bowl.
11. Check for the equality in the thickness of the walls with a double-ended caliper as you reduce the insides of the bowl. Go down by an inch at a time so that the edges are always backed up by some stock.
12. You can leave a bit of a nub at the bottom.
13. Place a piece of router mat over the insulations. Then, place the bowl over the mat and bring up the tailstock for support.
14. To remove the spigot at the bottom, you need a slight touch of the tool at that area until you are left with something that can still hold on to the bowl. You can add lines and coves to the bottom of the bowl.
15. Sand the bottom of the bowl while making sure you do not apply too much pressure.
16. Leave the bowl in the jam chuck and use a gouge to remove the nub left at the bottom. Sand it to your liking.
17. Apply Tung oil to the surface of the project. Allow it to dry for some hours.

18. You are done!

Faceplate Turning an End-Grain Hollow Vessel

Supplies

- Roughing gouge.
- ½″ bowl gouge.
- Skew chisel.
- Parting tool.
- Round nose scraper.
- Hollowing tool and hollow calipers.
- Four-jawed chuck.
- Jacobs chuck with a drill bit of an inch diameter.
- Use any wood of your choice—4″ by 4″ by 9″.

- Sanding pads and sandpapers of different grits.
- A lathe device with its speed set between 500 and 2000rpm.
- Tung oil.

Procedure

1. Reduce the square stock to round cylindrical stock with a roughing gouge and a skew chisel.
2. Use a parting tool to make a spigot on each end of the round stock so that it can take the opening of the four-jawed chuck.
3. If you encounter cracks in the woodblock as you reduce it, don't worry. Just continue to cut through the wood until you no longer see the cracks.
4. Sand the outside of the vessel using the power sanding method.
5. For minor cracks in the wood, fill them up with some CA glue and sawdust to prevent the crack from elongating.
6. Reverse the vessel and place it in a four-jawed chuck. Adjust the vessel in the four-jawed chuck to see that the piece is well balanced

7. Once the four-jawed chuck properly secures the vessel, you can use a parting tool to remove the spigot left on the top of the project.

8. Insert a ½" drill bit into the Jacobs Chuck and drill the center of the vessel. To ensure that the walls don't crack, they should have the same thickness as the bottom of the vessel.

9. To check for the penetration of the drill bit, use a piece of dowel and a straight stick.

10. Get rid of the dowel and the stick and then place them at the top of the vessel to see the depth at which the drill bit penetrated the wood.

11. With a round nose scraper, hollow out the piece from the center of the hole you made with the drill bit to the outer edge of the vessel. Cut through the wood lightly to avoid catches.

12. As you bore through the vessel, it may get more difficult to control the scraper. Move the tool rest inside the vessel to help in keeping the scraper just above the piece's centerline. You might need a source of lighting to see the insides of the vessel.

13. The thickness of the wall should be fixed at this time when you begin to scrape the inside of the

piece. If you are consistent with the wall's thickness, there's a lesser chance of the block cracking.

14. You might need a special hollowing tool, depending on the opening you have made. Ensure that a tool rest supports the straight portion of this tool.

15. The hollowing tool should cut through the wood in small bites. Start from the inside and end at the outer edges. See that the curved part of the tool does not come in contact with the tool rest.

16. Continue to remove wood from the inside of the project while checking out often for the thickness of the walls.

17. Once the walls have equal thickness and depth, remove the vessel and reverse chuck it into the four-jawed chuck.

18. Use a bowl gouge to get rid of the spigot left at the bottom of the vessel.

19. You can finish the surface of your project with Tung oil.

Wood Bangles

Supplies

- A four to six-inch diameter disc
- Chuck jaws.
- Lathe device.
- Sandpaper.
- Sanding pads

Procedure

1. You could get wood from your bin of scrap wooden pieces. The size of whatever you get

depends on the size of the bangle you are making. The thickness of the bangle also depends on the thickness of your chuck jaw.

2. Make cross outlines at each edge of the wood to get the center. Mark the center and then bore a hole through it for your lathe's chuck.

3. Cut the corners to make it easier to start cutting the stock to shape.

4. Flatten the wood stock and turn it roughly to form a circular stock.

5. With a sharpened parting tool, make a rough cutting of the internal diameter of the bangle. You can make the cuttings about ¾" deep.

6. Remove the wood stock from the screw. Then, remove the screw from the lathe.

7. Insert the jaws of the new hole and then tighten the chucks.

8. To get rid of the insides of the bangle, mark the radius of the inner circle and use a parting tool to finish the cuts. The sharper the tool you use, the less sanding you need to make your project neater.

9. Sand the insides of the bangle while making sure to be careful with the chuck jaws. You can sand the insides with sandpaper of about 220 grits.
10. Smoothen the outer edges of the bangle and then part it from the block.
11. Sand the rest of the bangle's edges manually with sandpaper as that will work to get rid of the scratches. You could also use the sanding pad to get rid of the tiny scratches.
12. You can finish your bangle with a coating of wax.
13. You are done!

Wooden Rings

Supplies

- Scrap wood—either Maple or Hickory. 1½" by 1½" by ½".

- A lathe machine.
- Jacobs chuck.
- A ¼″ drill bit.
- A ¾″ drill bit.
- A jam chuck.
- Sanding paper.
- Sanding pad.

Procedure

1. Get a piece of junk wood that is larger than the one you are using for the ring. It will help you hold the ring in place as you use the lathe.
2. The next thing to do is drill a perfect hole for the finger that wants to wear it. To do this procedure, use the Jacobs chuck drill.
3. If you are making a large hole, you could drill out a pilot hole. This kind of hole will allow a bit of a larger diameter through the piece. Start with a ¼″ bit and finish with a ¾″ bit. You could also use a drill press for this operation.
4. Insert the ring on the spindle so that it holds it firmly enough for you to turn it around and then shape it.

5. If the ring blank is gripped too tightly, it may end up just breaking into two. If it's too loose, the ring could fall off. Check out the size of the ring blank as many times as possible. Stop when it fits just right in the spindle.

6. Turn the ring to the shape you want. Make sure you make slow and light cuts through the wood when it is rotated at high speed by the lathe machine. After this process, sand the edges.

7. When you are done with the above procedure, part it in any direction you want. Sand the edges again with sandpaper of 400-grits.

8. Finish the rings with wax or other oil finishes.

Weed Pots

Supplies

- A lathe device.
- A bowl gouge.
- Sandpaper up to 320 grits.
- Jacobs chuck.
- ¼" brad point drill bit.
- ½" drill bit.
- A round nose scraper.
- Tung oil.
- Mineral spirits.

Procedure

1. Get a woodblock that fits the size of the weed pot you want to make. For this project, Ashwood was used. It dries nicely and doesn't have splinters when cracked.

2. With a band saw, cut out flat edges that are parallel to one another. These two flats are for the drive spur and the live center, and then, you would need to form a mortise on the stock for the clamps to hold on to for grip.

3. Drive the spur through the mortise you formed and then mount it on the chuck. For more

support during the whole shaping process, you could push up the tailstock.

4. Tighten the tailstock into a position for you to be able to cut more smoothly.

5. Roughen the edges of the stock with a bowl gouge until you get the desired final shape. Once you do that, you can remove the tailstock and then position the tool rest on the face of the pot.

6. Sand the surface of the weed pot with sandpapers up to the 320-grit. You could also use sanding pads that will work to get rid of the tiniest scratches.

7. To bore a hole in the piece, fix your Jacobs chucks to the tailstock of your lathe device after screwing a ¼" brad point drill bit into its mouth. When you work this drill to the depth you want, you can then move on to the ½" drill bit.

8. To sand the top of your weed pot, use a round nose scraper to make the mouth concave. To follow this technique, work through the hole you formed with the drill bit. Sand the surface of your project up to 400-grit and then apply a finish of your choice.

9. Here, Tung oil was used and because it was in its pure form, it was diluted with mineral spirits and polyurethane.
10. When the finish dries off, part the project from the tailstock and then wax the surface to protect the projects from moisture.

Letter Opener

Supplies

- A spindle roughing gouge.

- A spindle gouge.
- A parting tool.
- A skew chisel.
- A Jacobs-type chuck.
- A 5″ sanding disc holder.
- 1″ or 2″ sanding drum.
- Sandpaper of 80-grits, 120-grits, 150-grits, and 220-grits.
- A 220-grit sandpaper for the sanding disc.
- A 100-grit sleeve for the sanding drum.

Procedure

1. Start with a 1¼″ square of wood that has an approximate length of 10 inches. Mount the blank on the lathe device and turn it into a cylindrical stock with a spindle roughing gouge.
2. Know where the handle will move to form the blade. See that the portion for the blade is longer than the one for the handle. Divide the length equally for the beads. Separate the handle of the opener from the blade area by rolling a bead. Cut in with a parting tool or a skew chisel. Roll the bead with a spindle gouge.

3. To make the letter opener, shape the portion of the blade to look like an asymmetrical ellipse while using a skew chisel or detail gouge. Most letter openers usually swell from the tip so the blade portion has to resemble an ellipse.

4. Shape the handle into something that will give you a comfortable grip. You can try out several designs or shapes for this stage.

5. You can choose to leave the handle either detailed or smooth. Small beads would do well to improve the grip and if you want to make them, try to vary their sizes for ornate reasons. Here, the beads were wider in the middle and narrow at the end. Layout the series of beads with the long point of the skew chisel. To roll the beads, use a spindle gouge.

6. Sand the whole project except the blade area with sandpaper of 220-grit. Remove the letter opener from the ends of the lathe device and cut the waste material at the end with a coping saw. You could also use a skew chisel to part the letter opener from the headstock.

7. Shape the blade by sanding it. To reduce the wood dust, cut the waste wood with the coping

saw while the letter opener is still mounted on the lathe device. Position a dust collection system by the headstock and make sure you wear an effective dust mask.

8. Mount the Jacobs chuck in the headstock to be fixed with the 5″ sanding disc holder with sandpaper of 80 grits attached to it. Work the blade to its basic shape. Start from the middle to the outer edges to create a double-sided wedge. For an opener to function effectively, ensure that the edges of the blade are fairly sharp. The 80-grit sandpaper cuts too strongly, so switch to the 100-grit. As you get closer to the final shape, switch to the 120-grit. To finish the disc sanding, use the 220-grit.

9. Finish the blade by sanding it manually while making sure to follow the grain.

10. Make sure that the knife's blade is short and cylindrical.

11. As you turn the handle, stop during the process and see how it feels when you grip it.

12. Use a sanding drum to add beautiful highlights to the drum.

13. You could use a gel varnish if you want a film-forming finish. For an oil finish, use Tung oil or linseed oil. For protection against stains, use pure mineral oils or walnut oil.

14. You are done!

Ice Cream Scoop

Supplies

- Hardwood like Maple or Cherry.
- Spindle detail gouge.
- Sandpaper of different grits like the 320-grit, 400-grit, or the #0000 steel wool.
- Drill chuck.
- Parting tool.
- Outside calipers.

Procedure

1. For the scoop's handle, use a dense wood. Start by drilling a hole for the scoop's stem at the end of the handle's blank.

2. You could also drill the hole with a lathe machine. This technique requires that you turn the blank into a cylinder. Replace the tailstock's center with a drill chuck. The mark left by the tailstock center locates the bit.

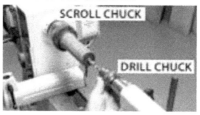

3. Once you have drilled the hole, you can re-mount the blank in two different ways. You can use a

cone-shaped live center or a small tapered plug. The cone centers itself, and the plug fills the hole so that you can mount a standard live center.

4. Turn the tenon to house the scoop's ferrule in two steps. First, match the ferrule's outer diameter. Then, reduce the diameter until you can drive on the ferrule.

5. Once you have driven on the ferrule, shape the area behind it with a spindle detail gouge while working from small to large diameters. You could start with a wide tapered flange.

6. Reduce the diameter behind the flange to create the neck. From this point on, remove the handle often to check how it feels when you grip it.

7. Start shaking the end of the handle. Leave enough waste, so you don't whack into the chuck.

8. Use a skew chisel to finish shaping the handle's rounded areas. You can also shape the entire

handle with a spindle detail gouge, but then, the skew chisel makes better outlines.

9. Trim the end of the tenon flush with the ferrule. Use the skew chisel with the long-end down or use a thin-kerf plating tool.

10. Finish the handle by sanding it. Start with a 120-grit and if you still see the turning marks, go back to using the 100-grit. Work your way up till you get to the 220-grit. Sand the brass ferrule to the sane grit.

11. Use finishes like polyurethane if you need the scoop to be protected from water. While finishing, sand in between each layer with a 320 grit sandpaper or a #0000 steel wool. For a natural look, use linseed oil.

Wooden Plate

Supplies

- A lathe device.
- A faceplate.
- A bowl gouge.
- Spindle gouge.
- A square-ended scraper.

Procedure

1. Mount the band saw blank for turning. The back of the plate will be turned first, so fix the faceplate on the blank's front. The screw holes disappear when the front side of the plate is shaped.

2. Use a bowl gouge to align the edges of the blank and then make it round. Make sure you don't splinter the blank's faces by working the edges from both sides. Start from the outside and move to the center.

3. Flatten the back sure of the blank. Work from the center to the outer edges. Start with a bowl gouge first and then proceed to use a square-ended scraper to level the surface.

4. Use a straightedge to check the leveled surface. The central area must be flat so you can easily remount the faceplate when it is time to turn the plate's open side.

5. Use the bowl gouge to shape the backside of the rim. Work from small to large diameter. As you shape the outside, consider your intention for the inside shape.

6. Mark a circle on the spinning blank. Make sure it is slightly larger than the faceplate. Remove the blank from the lathe and the faceplate from the blank.

7. Remount the faceplate on the outside of the blank, using the central circle and a high-strength

double-faced tape. Trim the tape to match the faceplate.

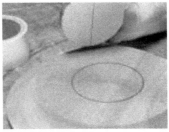

8. Remount the blank, then use the tailstock and a block to clamp the taped joint. The block is not glued as it is used to distribute the clamping pressure.
9. Sand the back of the rim using a cushioned disc and a drill set to rotate it clockwise. Before sanding, remove the clamp block and reposition the tailstock so that it continues to support the plate.
10. Always work from the outer edges to the middle when shaping the open side of the blank. Start by creating the rim. You can make it flat, curved, or detailed. Here, cutting in with a parting tool roughens a bead out.

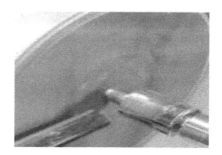

11. Roll the bead with a spindle gouge. Complete each side separately by starting at the center and working to the edge.

12. Remove the waste beyond the rim with the bowl gouge. Plunge down and towards the center with the bowl gouge. This step allows you to complete the rim.

13. The rim can be tapered, flat, wide, or narrow. It all depends on what you want and the shape you created outside the plate.

14. Establish the depth of the plate. Cut in from the edge of the trim by plunging down and towards the center.

15. Get rid of the waste at the center using the opposite side of the gouge and working in the opposite direction. Plunge in and down to full depth. To complete this stage, remove it from the tailstock.

16. Make a light cut with the bowl gouge to blend the transition between the two cuts. Switch to a square-ended scraper to level the surface. Then, finish this side of the plate.

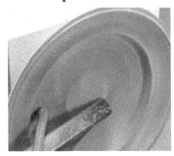

17. Remove the plate from the faceplate slowly and steadily. Remove any tape or residue that remains with mineral spirits. Finish the back of the plate by sanding manually.
18. Apply a finish of Tung oil to the surface of the plate.
19. You are done!

Spinning Tops

Supplies

- A lathe machine.
- A narrow parting tool.
- A spindle detail gouge.
- A skew chisel.
- A spindle roughing gouge.

- ¼″ drill bits.
- Jacobs chuck
- Scroll chuck.

Procedure

1. Use the tailstock center to hold the blank for the disc-shaped top bodies in position as you tighten the scroll chuck.

2. Round the edges of the blank with a spindle roughing gouge.

3. Cut in with the narrow parting tool to establish the disc.

4. Center a tiny recess in the disc's face.

5. Use the recess and a Jacobs-type chuck mounted in the tailstock to drill a hole through the disc. The hole must be centered accurately for the top to spin without wobbling.

6. Shape the body as you would roll a bead by starting at the edge. Cut towards the center rotating the gouge as you go. When shaping the back, don't cut to the central hole.

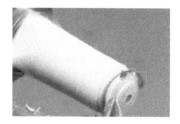

7. Create an interesting texture with a chatter tool. A chatter tool vibrates when it comes in contact with the wood, causing the tips to leave snuggly marks on the wood's surface.

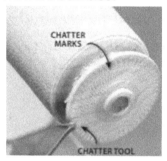

8. To chatter the tip of the body, move the tool rest back and hold the chatter tool as shown below. Start near the center and draw the tool towards the edge

9. Emphasize the chatter marks with color. Use delicate touches to color the high points and then sand lightly to remove the color from those points.

10. Free the project by cutting through the hold with a narrow parting tool. Catch the project in your hand as it falls.

11. To finish turning the bottom face, turn it around and remount it on a stub spindle that you've turned on a scrap block.

12. Complete the bottom face with light cuts and finish sanding.

Heirloom Awl

Supplies

- A lathe machine.
- A spindle or detail gouge.
- 1/64″ drill bits.

- Abrasive discs.
- Sanding paper of different grits.
- Locking pliers.
- Electric drill.
- A propane-fueled gas touch.
- Olive oil.
- Jacobs-chuck.
- Scroll chuck.
- Epoxy.

Procedure

1. Round the handle blank and fit the ferrule at the end of the stock. You can use other materials for the ferrule. Here, a solid grass nut with a tapered end section was used.

2. Rough-in the basic shape of the handle with the detail gouge. The shape and the size of the handle is something you determine.

3. Turn the flats of the nut away and shape the ferrule with a detailed gouge. Cutting brass and copper on the lathe device is very similar to cutting through wood. However, see that you take light cuts.

4. Drill the hole that will take in the steel drill rod. Use bits that are about $1/64$ inches larger in diameter than the drill rod to allow room for the epoxy.

5. Make the owl's steel shaft from a piece of drill rod. Cut it to length using a hacksaw
6. Shape the tapered point on the shaft with a drill and a lathe mounted abrasive disc. With the drill running, grind the point on the near lower quadrant of the spinning disc.
7. Harden the shaft by heating the pointed half to an even cherry rod color. Hold the shaft in a pair of locking pliers.
8. When the steel is evenly bright red from the point to the middle, quickly quench and stir it in a can of olive oil.
9. Test the hardness of the shaft by running it along with the file. The hardened part should skate off the file, not bite in.

10. Sand the steel to a bright, clean surface with 220-grit sandpaper. To remove the oil residue, wash the surface with soap and water.

11. Temper the shaft with a torch held just below the heat-treated area. Keep the flame there and rotate the shaft until the hardened area is a uniform dark gold or bronze color. After, douse the flame with water.

12. Set the shaft in the handle using a bit of slow set epoxy. Insert the epoxy in the hole with a toothpick. Rotate the shaft a bit to distribute the epoxy regularly.

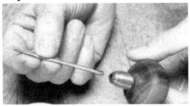

13. You are done.

Reading Glass Case

Supplies

- A lathe machine.
- 1½" by 9" by 10" square block of wood.
- A spindle roughing gouge.
- A spindle gouge.
- A parting tool.
- A skew chisel.
- A scroll chuck.
- Forstner drill bits.

Procedure

1. Start by cutting out tenons on both ends of the blank. You will need these tenons later when you drill out the cap and the base.

2. Separate the cap from the base by cutting in with a parting tool. Stop before you cut through the grip. Twist the blank to break the pieces apart.

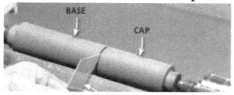

3. Drill out the cap with a Forstner's bit attached to the extension for deep drilling and an adaptor for mounting the tailstock. Advance the tailstock slowly to move the bit into the spinning blank.

4. Face off the cap's rim by scraping the surface with a skew chisel. The rim must be flat or tapered slightly to the inside. Mark the depth of the drilled hole on the blank.

5. Follow the same procedure to drill out the base. Use a Forstner bit to drill a hole that's of a diameter of 2/38" deep.

6. Turn the tenon on the base to fit the hole in the cap. Start with oversized holes and then reduce the diameter to create a tight fit. A cone center supports the drilled out ends.

7. Mount the cap and ensure that the assembled joints do not slip and that the ends of both drilled

holes are marked. Bring up the cone center to support the end of the reassembled mark.

8. Turn the case to the cylinder after fixing the ends by cutting in with the parting tool about ¼" beyond each tool mark.

9. Create a tactile surface and disguise the joint by adding decorative details such as beads.

10. Round the end of the cap by making rolling cuts with the spindle gouge. Finish the cap and the base by sanding the surfaces.

11. Use the skew chisel to part the cap, remove the cap from its base, and finish it by sanding it again.

12. Tune the joint's fit by removing a tiny amount from the tenon with a peeling cut. You'll hear a vacuum pop when you release the cap.

13. You are done.

Chapter 6

Common Woodturning Mistakes to Avoid

- Sanding in a direction opposite the grain lines of wood is one wrong thing to do. When you mount your wood stock on the roaring lathe, do not just hold the sandpaper to it as it turns. This way, you could probably be going across the grain lines and this makes scratch marks very visible. Before you use sandpaper of finer grit, make sure you power off the lathe first and then, take note of the grain lines. Then, follow these lines to prevent the incident of scratches. Scratches that flow with the grain lines are usually not visible.

- Practicing on softwood can be very bad. Softwood may be cheaper than hardwood but then, turning with it might not be enjoyable. Softwood is usually hard to turn as it is susceptible to cracks and chippings under the action of cutting tools. Hardwood requires very sharp tools and that will fetch you wonderful results.

- Turning at the wrong speed will fetch you bad results. When turning large and unbalanced wood stocks, make sure the lathe works at slow speeds. Moving at a quick pace can be very dangerous as the stock could spin out of the clamp's grip. Going slowly can also help you to make perfect cuts in wood.

- Turning with dull tools will fetch you bad outlines on your projects. Sharpening your tools isn't all too enjoyable, but then, cutting with blunt tools can be much worse. It exposes the project to the risk of tear-outs and catches.

- Did you re-tighten your chuck after the first time? This technique is tied to most 4-jaw chucks. After tightening it once, you may have to do it again to make sure that it's tight enough to hold down your wood stock. Just lock it tight and spin in a bit to see how tight the lock is.

- Did you weigh down the lathe? Mini lathes are not usually big or heavy, so to fight the issue of vibration, make sure they are tied to something bigger than them. If you do not follow this procedure, the turning of your wood piece might be rough as it doesn't stay much at a point.

- Not wearing protective instruments could be very risky. Do not look down on the importance of any protective gear. Wood scraps spinning off a lathe can be very dangerous if it hits your body.

- Do not make the mistake of not repositioning the tool rest as you do your projects.

The end... almost!

Hey! We've made it to the final chapter of this book, and I hope you've enjoyed it so far.

If you have not done so yet, I would be incredibly thankful if you could take just a minute to leave a quick review on Amazon

Reviews are not easy to come by, and as an independent author with a little marketing budget, I rely on you, my readers, to leave a short review on Amazon.

Even if it is just a sentence or two!

So if you really enjoyed this book, please...

\>\> Click here to leave a brief review on Amazon.

I truly appreciate your effort to leave your review, as it truly makes a huge difference.

Chapter 7

Woodturning Frequently Asked Questions

- **What kind of lathe can be used for the wooden bowls?**

Wooden bowl lathes are suitable for turning bowls; however, they are not different from other lathe devices. One thing that favors them is the lack of a bed rail fixed to the bed of the lathe. This way, you can have enough access to a bowl at all times.

- **How many tools do I need to turn a wood bowl?**

You will need a bowl gouge, a four-jawed chuck, a lathe device, a faceplate, and measuring tools like calipers and depth gauges.

- **Why does my bowl's wooden stock keep falling off the four-jawed chuck?**

This issue may be because the tenon or mortise in the wood stock was not formed rightly. Always take your time to make a mortise in your wood stock. You should also make use of dovetail angles that match your 4-jaw chucks. Avoid using serrated or toothed chuck jaws.

The tenon should also not have any contact with the bottom of the chuck. The tenon shoulder needs to lie flush on the top of the jaws.

- ▪ **Why should I get bowl gouge chips?**

First, you need to check the angle the bowl gouge is inclined to. To prevent the issue of catches, use a marker to mark the area of the flute on the bowl gouge. So, with this mark, you will know when the gouge is at an angle that will lead to the fibers getting caught.

- ▪ **What can I use to finish my bowls?**

If the bowl is to be used for food, use finishes like lemon oil or Tung oil. If the bowl isn't for food, you can use cellulose sealants, beeswax, and other oil finishes.

- ▪ **How can I season a log of timber?**

Timber can be seasoned by drying it in a microwave, kiln, or by air-drying it. Drying your wood in a kiln will usually give you the best result as it will help you get rid of most of the moisture. Air-drying a log of wood will only suck out moisture to the point of the atmosphere's temperature and if every where's humid, this technique might not be the best.

- **How can I check how much moisture is trapped in my wood?**

Moisture meters work best for this purpose. The inexpensive type has two teeth-like structures that you have to push through the wood to know the moisture content. The cheap meter is usually placed on a flat surface to get a reading. Depending on what you want to use the timber for, there are several moisture content readings.

A rating of 8% means the wood is too dry.

A rating that falls between 8% and 10% means you can use the wood stock for furniture.

A rating that falls between 10% and 15% means that you can use the wood stock for most woodturning projects.

A rating between 15% and 20% is for any turned item that is fit for warping.

A rating of 20% shows a high moisture content. This kind of content means that the wood stock is susceptible to cracks.

- **How do I get my projects to have smooth surfaces?**

Sand your pieces with a series of sandpaper, with each of different grits. Start with the ones with low grits and work your way to the higher ones. You could also apply finishing oils with high sheen across the surfaces of the project

- **Why do my wood projects change over time?**

All wood stocks react to light, humidity levels of the atmosphere, and heat. So, try to protect the pieces from those factors. Once you add wax and other sheening agents, all you need to do to retain the sheen is constant polishing and dusting.

Conclusion

Woodturning is an art that involves carving out wood to form beautiful pieces of structures and the outline in this book meticulously describes the steps involved in creating them. Apart from the tips you have read in this book, it would help if you also worked with a lot of confidence. Seeing a lathe device rotate at a very high speed can easily intimidate anyone, but then, you can be sure to attack this issue with a well of confidence. You should also be patient while working with a lathe device. Don't push too hard, or you could get frustrated quite quickly.

Regarding the projects outlined herein, repeat the procedures repeatedly to ensure that you can work fluidly without making too many errors.

Constant practice prevents poor performances.

Happy turning, woodturners!

Lightning Source UK Ltd.
Milton Keynes UK
UKHW021832020122
396528UK00003B/347